High Tides, Low Tides

High Tides, Low Tides
The Story of Leroy Colombo

Jean F. Andrews

LAMAR UNIVERSITY press

ISBN: 978-0-9850838-2-3
Library of Congress Control Number: 2013947027
Photos courtesy of Rosenberg Library and Texas
School for the Deaf

Manufactured in the United States of America

Lamar University Press
Beaumont, Texas

For Jerry Hassell
(1928 – 2007)
Reading teacher
Advocate of the Deaf Community
and Friend of Leroy Colombo

Other Books from Lamar University Press

Acknowledgments

This work of nonfiction is based on interviews, photographs, reports in books and journals, and my experiences working in the Deaf community for the past 30 years. For their guidance and help, I thank Russ Colombo, Mike and Pauli Gaido, Dr. Jim Marquette, and Don Mize. Don who died unexpectedly was a teacher, historian and friend who supplied me with numerous historical documents, contacts and encouragement. I also thank the late Jerry Hassell to whom I dedicated this book because he cared so much about Leroy's legacy for Deaf youth. I thank other members of the Deaf community I interviewed: Early McVey, Marcus Kleberg, Franna Camenisch, and Richard Norton. I thank Vic Maceo, Bill Scott and Sidney Steffans—members of the Galveston Beach Patrol—for sharing lifeguard stories and memories about Leroy. For their help with my research, I thank Carol Wood and Casey Greene of the History Archives in the Rosenberg Library. I also read accounts of Leroy from the Deaf community's point of view, contained in Deaf periodicals at the Gallaudet University Archives.

Writing Leroy's story was a challenge because there were gaps in the documentation of his early years. In writing about those years, I conjectured about his family's response to his deafness and their decisions for his education. Some of these conjectures were based on the understanding of Deaf education of the time. Also, in writing about Leroy's life at the Texas School for the Deaf, I drew upon information in Sharon Hovinga and Franna Camenisch's fascinating history: *Texas School for the Deaf Sesquicentennial: A Proud Tradition*.

I also thank the graduate students at Lamar University who assisted me in my research: Elaine Boland, Rachel

Graham, Dr. Charles Katz, Dr. Ying Li, Dr. Cynthia Hargreaves Shaw, Dr. Adonia Smith and Deanna Terro. Finally, I thank my editors Dr. Dennis Vail and Jennifer Ravey for their comments and Dr. James Phelan, my husband who listened to drafts and who suggested the title for this biography.

CONTENTS

1   Prologue: Tarzan of the Sea

11   Italian Roots

21   Becoming Deaf

33   Frustration

45   Beginnings at TSD (1915-1918)

59   First Save

65   More TSD (1918-1922)

73   Seawater Racer

85   Leroy and the History of Lifeguarding

93   Living and Working on the Beach

103   Rescues

117   Leroy's Deaf Community

125   Last Lap

135   Timeline

139   Bibliography

147   Book Club Discussion Questions

Why the word *deaf* in this book is sometimes written with a capital *D*

The editors at Lamar University Press accept the practices of capitalization adhered to by the Deaf community in the United States, as explained best by Tom Holcomb, author of *Introduction to American Deaf Culture*.

The term *Deaf* with a capital *D*, says Holcomb, refers to culturally Deaf people who use American Sign Language (ASL) and consider themselves part of the Deaf culture with its unique values, heritage and history, art, literature, behavioral norms and visual orientation to the world. When spelled with the lower case *d*, deaf refers to persons in the general population who have the audiological condition of being deaf but who neither use ASL nor belong to the Deaf culture.

Illustrations

xi   The Young Leroy Colombo

7   The Leroy Colombo Swim Center

15   Galveston Map, storm damage, seawall

115 The Mature Leroy Colombo

128 The Elder Leroy Colombo

133 Beach Memorial

Above: Leroy, far right, with friends in
Barton Springs, Austin

The Young Leroy Colombo

Colombo won
many swimming
races, even besting the famous
Johnny Weissmuller in one long
distance race.

Leroy on the shoulders of a fellow lifeguard

Prologue
Tarzan of the Sea

I must go down to the sea again, for the call of the running
    tide
Is a wild call and a clear call that may not be denied
           "Sea Fever," John Masefield

The warm April day had started calmly. It was 1945, and Galveston Beach was overrun with tourists. A middle-aged man with a paunch and leathery skin presided over the crowd. He wore red swim trunks, sunglasses, a white safari hat, and a metal whistle hanging around his neck—the standard-issue uniform of the volunteer Galveston Lifeguard Beach Patrol.

Leroy Colombo was 39 years old but still fit and handsome with his charming smile that disarmed many. As he squinted at the horizon, white pools of sea foam rushed about his feet.

That day, like other warm spring days in Galveston, dozens of women in cotton-flowered sun dresses and sun hats, children in sunbonnets, and men in baseball hats—all hauling umbrellas, chairs, and picnic baskets—made a trail from the seawall stairs onto the beach. Most had never had a swim lesson.

Leroy checked his imaginary safety line and the swimmers beyond it, and yelled, "Move in!" He blew his whistle and shouted again, in a gravelly voice, "Too damn deep!" But the din of the surf, seagulls, and people drowned out his warning.

The surf was rough. The wooden groins and piers were designed to break the strength of the waves, but they could do nothing to hold back the strong current that was moving in. Leroy had noted the red seaweed, the color of the algae, and the increased debris on the shore, knowing these were clues to rip currents, deadly swirls of saltwater that knocked many swimmers off balance, even in shallow water. Those in deeper water typically fought against the current until they succumbed to exhaustion, their heads dipping below the water before they drowned.

During his career, Leroy made more than 900 saves, according to Norris and Ross McWhirter in their *Guinness Book of World Records*. Leroy's abilities were legendary, and that day he was as strong and fit as ever.

Three heads bobbed in and out of the water, too far out to be safe. Leroy threw off his hat and sunglasses, grabbed a metal buoy, and raced into the surf. Immediately, a wall of salt water slapped him. He spit out the water and swam toward the pier.

Ahead, a woman in a red swimsuit grabbed the pier pulling herself against the barnacle-encrusted pier. The water around her turned red as she scratched her arms and legs against the sharp growths.

Another woman in a black swimsuit lost her grip. Her head disappeared below the water. Both women flailed about, desperately trying to hold on to the rough pilings.

Leroy pumped his legs in the water before diving and pulling up the first woman, holding her in a bear hug. A wave carried them both to shore. Back into the surf, he swam out, grabbed the other woman, and pulled her to safety using the metal buoy strapped to his shoulder. He swam parallel to the beach, moving skillfully out of the deadly current and allowing a wave to push them to shore.

Others gathered on the beach, and Leroy left the two women in the care of those on the shore. Leroy went back for the third swimmer, who was struggling.

The man clung to the pilings of the pier. As Leroy approached, the man slapped him sharply in the face. Leroy pushed him away, but the man slapped him again, flailing his arms as he struggled against the water and the waves. Leroy ringed one arm around the man's neck. The man was petrified with fear and refused to let go. Leroy grasped his leg and pushed him into a wave until the man went under and came up, gasping for air. Leroy grabbed him and scissor-kicked his way to shore. He deposited the man next to the two coughing women on the beach.

"Two of the woman were semi-conscious when they were rescued but revived without the aid of artificial respiration," reported *The Galveston Daily News*. All coughed and sputtered while onlookers wrapped the swimmers and Leroy in dry towels.

For most there, the noise of an ambulance and the gathering crowd was deafening. People talked and pushed, trying to get a look at the hero and the bedraggled survivors. But Leroy never heard a thing. Even in that din, the world around him remained silent. Leroy had not heard his own voice or any other noise since a childhood illness robbed him of his hearing at age six.

The three swimmers were put in the ambulance, and Leroy joined them. He liked to accompany those he rescued to the hospital. On occasions that Leroy witnessed the drowning victim's death at the hospital, he cried like a baby.

Later that day, Leroy pulled out of the surf a soldier near the same location as the women earlier in the day. The man was clinging precariously to the pilings under the municipal pier. Leroy pulled the soldier to shore.

That day, the four swimmers would live and not require hospitalization, with one victim suffering "only lacerations and bruises to the body as the surf rocked him against the pilings," according to a report in *The Galveston Daily News*. The report went on to say that Leroy saved "three Houston visitors and a West Virginia soldier from a strong outgoing undercurrent near the municipal pier yesterday afternoon." Over the years, Christie Mitchell and other hearing reporters from *The Galveston Daily News* referred to the Leroy in such terms as "the deaf and dumb eagle-eyed swimming marvel" and the man who "beat his chest in Tarzan-like fashion" who frequently saved tourists and locals from drowning.

When she was living, Leroy's mother proudly clipped each such article from the newspaper and placed them in a family scrapbook. The scrapbook still exists and today is housed in Galveston's Rosenberg Library.

But Leroy's story is not defined by that one sentimental family document. His legacy is highly visible; it can be measured in part by the many ways people have chosen to honor the man and to ensure future generations will remember him.

Born of Italian immigrant parents and raised on Galveston Island, Leroy was a highly accomplished lifeguard, diver and salt-water sea-racer. He was also a humanitarian, and in the time of segregation, he saved hundreds from drowning, regardless of race. He was skilled with a surfboard and, according to Kelly Hawes, a reporter for *The Galveston Daily News*, Leroy surfed the Galveston shoreline long before surfing became popular on the west coast. The Galveston community adored him for his athletic prowess as well as his lifesaving abilities. Members of the media loved him for the excitement and fame he brought to the island. Most of all Leroy was a hero in the Deaf community because of his outstanding accomplishments.

Nicknamed "Dummy Colombo" and called "deaf-mute," Leroy was not mute. He could speak, though he did so in a monotone voice that people had difficulty understanding. He carried a pad and pencil to communicate with strangers, and he was accomplished at lipreading, according to an article journalist Robert Jones published in the *In Between Magazine*.

Since his death almost 40 years ago, Leroy has not been forgotten. Many have contributed to keeping Leroy's name and legacy alive, including members of the Texas legislature, citizens of the city of Galveston, and faculty and administrators at the Texas School for the Deaf. Among the private citizens who worked to ensure Leroy's fame are Jerry Hassell, Richard Norton, Dr. Jim Marquette, A.R. (Babe) Schwartz and Donald Mize.

When Leroy died on July 12, 1974, the members of the Texas State Senate stood for a moment of silence in his honor for his service on Galveston beaches. Also, the city of Galveston passed a resolution on July 18, 1974 honoring Leroy Colombo: "Whereas, because of his dedication, heroism and valuable contributions to the city of Galveston, Mr. Colombo will always be remembered by the citizens of Galveston as one of its most outstanding citizens ...this Resolution be spread upon the Minutes of the City Council, July 18, 1974."

Still another honor bestowed on Leroy was by the Optimist Club who dedicated and installed a concrete and bronze marker on the Seawall and 51st Street. On the marker are these words: "In memory of Leroy Colombo, a deaf-mute who risked his own life repeatedly to save more than a thousand lives from drowning in the waters surrounding Galveston Island."

One year after his death, on April 25, 1975, the Texas Senate and Senator A.R. (Babe) Schwartz sponsored a senate resolution (S.R. No. 49) in the memory of Leroy Colombo and ordered the lowering of the state flag. The resolution read: "Whereas, the people of the city of Galveston were greatly saddened by the death on Friday, July 12, 1974, of the well-loved man who was called 'the Lifeguard of Galveston, Mr. Leroy Colombo; and... Resolved, that the Senate of the State of Texas, by this Resolution, express appreciation for the life and service of

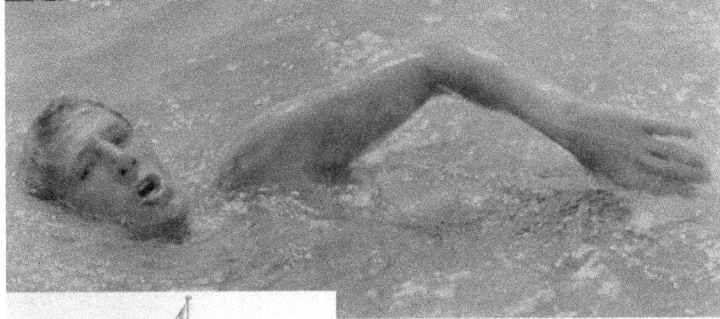

Top: Dedication of the Leroy
Colombo Swim Center in Austin,
Texas

Middle: the most famous photo of
Colombo swimming

Bottom: Leroy Colombo on the right

Leroy Colombo...and be it further Resolved, That copies of this Resolution be prepared for the members of his family, and that when the Senate adjourns today, it do so in memory of, and in tribute to, Mr. Leroy Colombo, April 25, 1975."

Leroy was inducted into the Texas School for the Deaf Athletic Hall of Fame in 2002. He joined the many other Deaf athletes who were students at the school and who excelled in sports. A picture of Leroy holding a swimming trophy hangs today in the Heritage House, the museum at the Texas School for the Deaf in Austin.

Another accolade after Leroy's death came from the faculty at the Texas School for the Deaf when, according to *The Texas School for the Deaf Sesquicentennial,* "Richard Norton approached Marvin Sallop, the superintendent and suggested that the new natatorium be named after Leroy Colombo." In 2004, Jerry Hassel approached Superintendent Claire Bugen and the Governing Board to recommend naming the new natatorium after Leroy. This required legislative approval. In 2004, in the Texas State Senate Concurrent Resolution No. 21, the Senate "Resolved, that the 79th Legislature of the State of Texas hereby approve and authorize the naming of the natatorium at the Texas School for the Deaf in Austin the Leroy Colombo Swim Center." The dedication of the new natatorium occurred in 2006 at the anniversary of Texas School for the Deaf's 150-year anniversary, and Jerry Hassell was there to cut the ribbon.

Still another honor was given to Leroy when in June 2005 the city of Corpus Christi exhibited memorabilia of

Leroy Colombo's history as a surfer at the Texas Surf Museum. While Leroy's racing and lifeguarding accomplishments are well documented, few know about his surfing prowess. According to Kelly Hawes, a reporter for *The Galveston Daily News*, the museum in Corpus Christi provides a display of records that shows how Colombo was a "pioneering surfer. He was among the first to ride surfboards at Galveston beaches."

Due to the efforts of Don Mize, a teacher and historian, Colombo received another posthumous honor when the Galveston city council, on May 20, 2008, voted unanimously to rename a two-block stretch of 57th Street "Leroy Colombo's View." According to Donald Mize, this was the area Leroy patrolled when working as a lifeguard. Mize also led a project to have the Texas Historical Commission create an historical marker in Leroy's honor. The marker, located outside of the Galveston Island Convention Center, was installed in 2008.

Both the Rosenberg Library in Galveston and the Deaf periodicals collection in the Gallaudet University Archives contain numerous news articles that document Leroy's story. Today his name is honored in an annual 5K Ducky Prendergast/Leroy Colombo race held each summer in Galveston. According to Jerry Hassell, his name is frequently brought up among Deaf Texans at homecomings for the Texas School for the Deaf, at Deaf reunions, sports events and at meetings of the Texas Association for the Deaf.

The faculty and students at the Texas School for the Deaf in Austin have started a surf club. Club members swim laps in a natatorium bearing Leroy Colombo's name, evidence that Leroy Colombo's legacy lives on, especially with young Deaf athletes.

1

Italian Roots

And a gray mist on the sea's face, and a gray dawn
    breaking…
                "Sea Fever," John Masefield

Leroy's mother and father emigrated from Italy to Galveston Island, Texas. According to Valentine Belfiglio in *The Italian Experience in Texas,* a combination of rapid industrialization in northern Italy and poor farming in the south drove many families to abandon their homeland and head to Texas. For many Italians, Galveston Island seemed the right place for building a better life. Galveston was the port of entry for thousands of immigrants who settled in Texas and the Southwest United States.

The federal government had set up an immigration station on Galveston's Pier 29. Here U.S. Customs officers examined the immigrants for diseases, checked baggage, and processed the new arrivals. While Galveston Island never became an Ellis Island in terms of numbers of immigrants, it did deal with hundreds of newcomers. Galveston leaders had hoped that they could build a large immigrant landing station similar to New York's Ellis Island, but that never happened.

Leroy's father, Peter Colombo (1863-1913) was born in Milan, Italy, and his mother, Catherine Gaido (1873-1944) was born in Torino, Italy. While many Italian immigrants became fishermen, barbers, shoe repairmen and proprietors of candy shops, meat markets, retail stores, and fruit stores, Leroy's father settled into the restaurant business, which was a good choice because of the tourists who came in large numbers to Galveston Island.

According to interviews with the Gaidos family and Leroy's nephew Russ Colombo, managing restaurants ran in Leroy's ex-tended Italian family, the most successful restaurant being Gaido's Seafood Restaurant, which is still in operation today. Catherine, Leroy's mother, was the sister of San Jacinto (Cinto) Gaido (1886-1939). Cinto was the youngest of six children born to Giuseppe and Antonina Grosso Gaido. In 1888, he was only two years old when his widowed mother brought Cinto and his older brothers and sisters from Italy to be with family in Galveston. Shortly thereafter, Cinto's mother died, and Cinto was placed in an orphanage. His older sister Catherine was only 15 years old when their mother died. She took her young brother out of the orphanage and helped to raise him. Cinto, like other boys his age, started work early and had little formal education.

In their later years, Cinto and his wife Josephine promoted beachfront businesses in Galveston. Their restaurant started as a seafood canteen in 1911, called Gaido's Café, located on Murdock's Pleasure Pier.

Murdock's Pier later became the scene of many of Leroy's heroic rescues.

After several damaging hurricanes, this humble café moved across the street where it metamorphosed into an elegant restaurant with highly trained chefs and a varied menu of seafood dishes served on white tablecloths by waiters and waitresses in formal black and white attire. Uncle Cinto became an influential force in Catherine and Leroy's life for years to come. He even hired the young Leroy to flip hamburgers at his café and to wait on tables.

Leroy's mother, Catherine, became a nurse. In her early twenties, she had a job on Pelican Island, a small island on Galveston Bay that was used as a hospital and as an immigrant station. One day, two men brought in an injured man on a stretcher. His name was Peter Colombo. He had a badly infected wound in his abdomen from an arrow. He had emigrated from Italy, and he came into the U.S. to Pelican Island through Mexico. It was on the last part of his journey that an Indian shot him with an arrow.

After the doctor cleaned and dressed the wound, he assigned Catherine to watch the new patient. She changed his bandages daily until Peter Colombo got better. The nurse and the young Italian discovered they had much in common, especially their Italian heritage and their Catholic faith. Soon they fell in love. The ten-year difference in their ages did not seem to matter, at least during their early years of marriage.

After a brief courtship, Peter and Catherine had a wedding with a nuptial Mass at St. Mary's Cathedral. Food, wine, relatives and well-wishers were plentiful at the ceremony, and the Colombo couple settled in to family life.

In the Catholic tradition of the time, the couple

began to reproduce rapidly, baby after baby. Fortunately for Catherine, her body handled the frequent childbirths well. Many women died during this era from the strain of childbearing.

Galveston city birth records show that three of Leroy's brothers and sisters were born around the time of the 1900 hurricane that devastated Galveston. No records exist to tell how the Colombo family survived or even if they evacuated to another city. Historian David McComb wrote in *Galveston: A History*, "No one knows for sure how many people died on Galveston Island and the mainland—probably 10,000 to 12,000." The 1900 storm, McComb wrote, was "the most profound event in the lifetime of the city." After what is still the deadliest natural disaster in U.S. history, reconstruction and prevention became the goals of the city.

Five years before Leroy was born, and following the hurricane of 1900, the city of Galveston was in a flurry of activity. John Edward Weems wrote that sand was pumped in from the Gulf to add an additional three feet to the island. Houses, churches, schools, and stores began appearing again. Because of the overwhelming death toll and property damage from the storm, workers came from surrounding states, and many of them stayed to make Galveston their home. Amid all of this activity, Leroy's father found plenty of work to support his growing family.

Peter Leroy Colombo, a Christmas baby, was born on December 23, 1905 at St. Mary's Hospital, according to city birth records. Thus Leroy was BOI—Born on the Island. According to the Galveston culture, BOI citizens have more

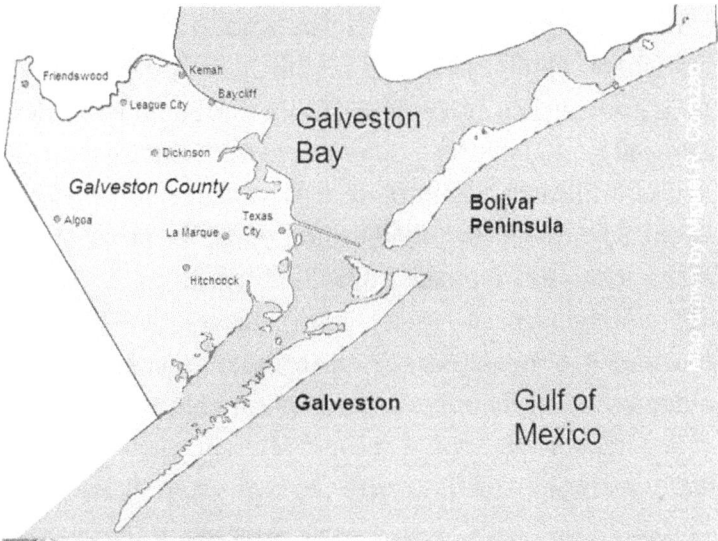

Leroy Colombo's parents, Peter and Catherine, survived the great storm of 1900 that devastated the island, and they stayed to help rebuild Galveston.

The Galveston seawall, built to avoid destruction from another hurricane, helped restore Galveston beach and bring tourists back to the island.

status and prestige than those who immigrate from elsewhere. One year before his birth, in anticipation of their growing family, Peter and Catherine bought a modest home at 1713 21st Street. City records of the house indicate it was built around 1890, so it must have survived the Great Storm of 1900, though no doubt like other structures, it suffered damage from the storm.

Arriving home as an infant, Leroy joined a busy household. Four sisters and one brother greeted him. His older sister, Lucie, most likely his first babysitter, was 11 years old, born in 1894. A second sister, Marie Antoinette, was 7 years old. The third sister, Esther, was only four, and Margaret would be born a year later, in 1901. Leroy's brother Christopher, called Nick, was three years old, born in 1903. Nick would become Leroy's closest ally, friend, and teacher for life, helping him through some difficult times warding off the loneliness of being the only deaf member of a large, caring family. Nick would help Leroy with financial and health challenges that plagued him throughout his life.

San Jacinto, nicknamed Cinto, Leroy's younger brother, was born in 1907. Then another sibling, Catherine, was born in 1909 and named after her mother. Leroy's mother spent most of her days doing family chores, breast feeding, cooking meals for her large family and forever changing, washing, drying and folding mountains of white cloth diapers.

All the Colombo children were baptized in the Roman Catholic Church, according to records in the Archdiocese of Galveston. Leroy received the sacrament of baptism on April 29, 1906 at St. Mary's Basilica Cathedral. For the Colombos, baptisms were much celebrated with rituals and family gatherings. One photo from his family's album shows Leroy dressed in a white lace baptismal dress, perhaps made by his mother or his Italian aunts.

Peter Leroy went by his middle name, Leroy, for his entire life. He and his brothers swam in the Gulf daily to improve their racing and swimming skills. Leroy's brothers defended him from the bullies in the neighborhood and school bullies who found Leroy easy prey because he could not hear what was going on around him. According to an interview with Russ Colombo, Leroy's nephew, all three Colombo boys—Leroy, Nick, and Cinto—were athletes who excelled at swimming in the Gulf and competed in races with each other throughout their boyhood

While growing up, the children found family life was not easy in the Colombo household. For Leroy's father, restaurant ownership and work was demanding and not stable enough to feed his large family. It required long hours and hard physical labor. Peter left the childcare and housekeeping to his weary wife, Catherine, while he changed jobs frequently, causing stress and tension in the family. Peter's health began to suffer.

For a time, the Colombo household was filled with eight children under the age of eighteen. All vied for their tired parents' attention and affection. Leroy's father worked 14 hours a day at the restaurant, six days a week. His mother worked around thee clock, forever holding at bay the dust, dirt, sticky fingerprints, muddy footsteps, dirty diapers, and greasy pots and pans which seemed to invade the household like a marching army.

As a young boy, Leroy played ball with his brothers and sisters and children from the neighborhood. His mother and father often took the family to the beach on the weekends, where Leroy played horseshoes and swam in the Gulf with Cinto and Nick and his sisters.

In the tradition of Italian Catholics at that time, after Sunday Mass at the Cathedral, the family often joined other extended family members for lunch. Leroy's father and uncles ate large Italian meals, then drank alcohol, played cards, smoked cigars and cut up with each other.

In many ways, Leroy's early years were idyllic, for he long remained unaware of the hard work of his mother and father, and he spent his days swimming and playing.

But when he turned six, he had a rude awakening. His parents enrolled him in school with his brothers and sister. Thereafter Leroy had to wear uncomfortable leather shoes and socks and clothes that itched and scratched his neck. School imposed a rigid routine on the young boy, causing him some distress, for already he had developed a carefree and independent spirit.

At the market one afternoon, Catherine stopped to talk to her neighbor. She learned that a strange disease had hit Texas and that many of Galveston's children were ill. Her neighbor said that one of the children down the street had just died from the new illness. She had seen the child's coffin draped in white at St. Mary's Cathedral, and she blamed "those foreigners" who brought strange diseases from Europe. Catherine made the sign of the cross, grabbed her groceries, and hurried away. She did not have the time to worry about strange diseases. She had laundry, meals to cook for eight hungry children and a tired and hungry husband to take care of.

One evening Peter and Catherine sat at the family dinner table, presiding over their noisy group of children who ate the stew and vegetables Catherine had cooked. Leroy, quieter than usual, played with his stew. After several bites, he vomited his stew on the tablecloth. His brothers and sisters laughed and began to imitate and mock him. Catherine told the children to quiet down.

She felt Leroy's head. It was hot. His heavy head drooped into his stew, then he jerked his head back and vomited into his mother's lap. Catherine ushered her young son to the bathroom to clean him up, then tucked him into bed. That night she watched over her son as he lay drifting in and out of sleep. She fell asleep in the chair next to him. The next morning she felt his head and was distressed to find it was even hotter. Worse, though, was her and Peter's inability to awaken Leroy. His breathing sounded congested, and he had sweated through the sheets.

Catherine remembered the conversation with her neighbor about strange diseases brought over by immigrants, but she tried to push it out of her mind. Can't happen to us, she told herself. But deep down, she was troubled, and her stomach felt tied in knots. She took out her rosary, said a few prayers, and dozed off beside her sick son with the beads still intertwined between her fingers.

2

Becoming Deaf

And all I ask is a tall ship and a star to steer her by…
"Sea Fever," John Masefield

Fog hung heavy in the air like ripe pears from a tree. A strong salty odor seeped into the house and clung to the rugs, furniture and curtains. Two worried parents leaned over Leroy.

For several days and nights, Leroy was sluggish. He moved little in his bed and refused to eat or drink. He was awake but confused, for he did not recognize his brothers and sisters as they slipped up to the side of his bed, peering at him. That evening, Leroy retched in dry heaves. There was little food or drink in his stomach. He shut his eyes against the light and covered his ears from the noises of the other children in the house.

Peter decided to call the family doctor.

When the doctor arrived in his Model T, with his black leather bag full of medicines and instruments, Catherine heaved a sigh of relief. Quickly she told the doctor of the symptoms that Leroy complained about, the headache, and the ache in his neck, the drowsiness. Catherine pointed to the pink rash that had slowly developed on Leroy's arms and legs. She sobbed. Through her crying, she asked the doctor if he would work a miracle and give Leroy some special medicine that would make him well.

The doctor nodded and washed his hands in a bowl Catherine had provided. He dried with a hand towel, then leaned over the bed to feel Leroy's forehead and held the boy's wrist to check his pulse. After listening to Leroy's heart with a stethoscope, the doctor glanced up at the parents' concerned faces and offered some advice: keep their feverish son cool with wet cloths to relieve his head-aches and stiff neck, feed him soup and water to keep him from becoming dehydrated.

The doctor motioned for Catherine and Peter to step outside. He smiled at Leroy's sisters, Lucie, Nettie, and Esther who, overhearing about the cold wet cloths, had brought one in and were playing nurse for their younger brother.

Outside the bedroom, the doctor spoke quietly so as to not alarm the children. He explained to Peter and Catherine that spinal meningitis had reached epidemic proportions in Texas over the past two years, and he explained that spinal meningitis is a swelling of the tissue around the spinal cord. Likely, the doctor said, Leroy had this disease. Blunt in his assessment, the doctor said that if a child survived spinal meningitis he could become paralyzed, deaf, blind, and epileptic.

Catherine put her hand over her face and began to cry in short, abrupt sobs. Peter put his arm around his wife.

"There is a possible medicine," the doctor said. Catherine wiped the tears from her face and looked hopefully at the doctor.

The doctor explained the medicine was a horse serum, one a Doctor Abraham Sophia had written about in the medical journals and *The New York Times*. The serum was supposed to be a cure for meningitis.

Leroy's doctor told his parents that good results were found using a serum that was taken from horses that had been injected with the disease. He went on to say that 90 percent of the patients who were not treated with the horse serum died. "The procedure is painful, though," he cautioned.

Peter and Catherine looked at each other. "We will do it," Peter said. Catherine put her hands in her apron, lowered her tired face and nodded.

That afternoon, the doctor returned. Peter ushered the other children out the door into the hands of a neighbor. He was not sure how his six-year-old son would respond to the injections.

When the doctor entered the room, he dropped his bag to the floor and got to work after washing and drying his hands. He filled one needle with the horse serum. Catherine and Peter stood at the other side of the bed. They held onto Leroy's arms as the doctor injected the long needle into the boy's lower spine. Leroy cried out in pain. Catherine put her arms around her son's head to comfort him, but he writhed away from her grasp and cried out again. Soon he stopped crying and drifted into a deep sleep.

The doctor placed his instruments into his bag, washed and dried his hands, and told Leroy's parents he would be back every 24 hours for a week. Catherine and Peter walked him to the door and thanked him.

Peter went back to work. Catherine sat up with Leroy every night for days, feeding him, giving him water and comforting him as he slipped in and out of sleep.

Years later when Leroy's friend Dr. Jim Marquette asked in an interview if Leroy had gone to the hospital, he replied, "No. Mama rocked me day and night. I had epileptic attacks."

Even with the serum treatment, Catherine and Peter feared their son's life was slipping away. One evening, Peter walked to St. Mary's Cathedral to ask the Monsignor to come to the house to give his son the Last Rites, the final sacrament that Catholics receive when they are dying. The Monsignor arrived and placed holy oil on the boy's forehead. His brothers and sisters and Peter and Catherine stood around the bed and prayed.

But miraculously and with the help of the serum, Leroy did not die. Slowly, after weeks in bed, he spent more hours awake than asleep. He asked for more food and water each day, and Catherine often surprised her son with his favorite foods.

One morning he was able to sit up in bed. His brothers and sisters were nearby playing on the floor in his bedroom. Leroy looked at Cinto and Nick fighting over a toy. But Leroy could not hear what they were saying. He saw their mouths moving, but no sounds were coming out. Then he looked at his sisters. Lucie sang a song to her doll.

Nettie, Catherine, and Esther sat nearby dressing and talking to their dolls. Leroy heard nothing. He shook his head and poked his fingers in his ears, but nothing changed.

Nick looked up and smiled. He threw a ball onto Leroy's bed, and it landed on his leg. Leroy tried to kick the ball back to Nick, but he could not move his leg. He tried both legs, but they were stiff and had no feeling. He cried out for his mother. She must not have heard him. He shouted again and again until his throat became hoarse. Catherine appeared at the door, flour clinging to her apron. She was baking his favorite, cherry pie.

Leroy pointed to his ears and shook his head. The tears spilled from his face as he pointed to his legs and cried out again.

When Peter arrived home late that night from the restaurant, Catherine told him what had happened. Peter recalled the doctor's warnings and attempted to comfort his wife, reminding her Leroy was still alive. Arms around each other, they walked to Leroy's room where they found the boy sound asleep, the covers thrown on the floor. Catherine picked up the blanket and gently tucked the boy in.

As the days turned into weeks Leroy regained strength, but he still could not hear or walk. At mealtime, Leroy's brothers and sisters even had to help him hold his fork because it would slip out of his fingers.

From his bed, Leroy could smell the salty air. He felt the breezes blowing in the window and saw the curtains moving. He noticed the pink oleanders in the front yard and wanted to pick a bouquet for his mother who had done so much for him since he was sick. He was tired of being sick. He wanted to get up and run around like before.

Propped up on his elbows, Leroy saw fronds of green palms moving, wind-driven and looking to be in slow motion, but could not hear their calming swishes as the wind blew them. He did not hear the gulls' calls that once awakened him each morning. Anger rose in him like steam. He felt he would explode any moment.

He wanted to be swimming at the beach with his brothers and catching the waves like they did before. He missed doing handstands in the sand and throwing the metal horseshoes, hearing the metal clang, signaling a bulls-eye. He missed watching the brown pelicans from high in the sky plunge diving into the Gulf for fish. He wondered if those small, silver fish still jumped in and out of the water or if the porpoises still paraded across the Gulf. He was stuck inside with legs that wouldn't move and ears that could not hear. Leroy was miserable.

Peter and Catherine felt tired, confused, and anxious. Catherine was impatient with the other children, distracted in her thoughts about Leroy. Peter worked long hours at the restaurant, and the children and Catherine only saw him occasionally. Peter and Catherine wanted desperately to help their son, but they did not know how or whom to turn to. They did not want to give up hope.

Gradually, Catherine, Peter and the brothers and sisters became accustomed to Leroy's gravelly, monotone voice. At first, Catherine stared at her son with sadness. But over time, the family accepted the changes in his voice and could even understand his new "deaf voice." The worried parents began talking to each other about finding a cure for Leroy's deafness. Maybe the doctor was wrong, they told each other.

Deciding it was time to take action, they found another doctor. According to Dr. McCay Vernon, psychologist, parents with newly diagnosed deaf children go through a "doctor shopping" phase, which amounts to a painful denial of the reality of permanent deafness.

Leroy's doctor suggested they rinse out his ears with salt water every day. This treatment proved successful only in giving Leroy earaches. They went to a second doctor. This doctor suggested they pour warm almond oil, honey and alcohol into the boy's ears. This treatment also failed to cure and caused Leroy much irritation. They went to a third doctor who suggested they place cooked onions and cabbage in his ears. This treatment did no more than make Leroy smell of cooked onions and cabbages for days. A fourth doctor suggested that Leroy drink lots of water to flush out his system. Leroy hated this treatment because it made him go to the bathroom so often. Finally Peter and Catherine gave up on the doctors.

Next they tried priests and nuns.

Dr. Vernon wrote that "religion can be a source of understanding and support, especially when devoutness is a part of deep, longstanding religious beliefs." Dr. Vernon cautions, though, "that religion can be an unhealthy reaction involving a miracle cure and an escape from reality, rather than a realistic adjustment to deafness."

As devout Catholics, Catherine and Peter approached

the parish priest for a cure, a religious miracle. The priest suggested the family take Leroy to the shrine of Our Lady of Guadalupe in Mexico where the Blessed Mother appeared to the humble peasant Juan Diego on the hill of Tepeyac, north of Mexico City. Rumored to heal those who came in supplication, the site drew many pilgrims. But the Colombos could not afford to take Leroy to Mexico. That night, Catherine and Peter and seven children knelt beside Leroy's bed. Peter led the family in a novena, a set of nine repetitive prayers that showed their devotion to the Blessed Mother Mary. Each day for nine days they said these prayers. After they finished the novenas, the family said a rosary to petition God and the Blessed Mother Mary for miracles. Prayer, they believed, was cheap but powerful.

One day at his restaurant Peter's co-worker suggested another cure. If Peter took Leroy up in an airplane, the change in air pressure would open Leroy's ears and restore his hearing. Peter could not wait to go home and tell Catherine and Leroy.

After he told her the news, Catherine cried out in joy and hugged her husband. They would take the extra cash they had saved for emergencies, and Peter would hire a pilot to take his son up into the clouds, up into heaven, really, where both God and the air pressure would work together and cure Leroy's deafness, or so they hoped and expected.

His father talked slowly to Leroy and explained that soon they would go up in an airplane. His mother repeated what Peter had said because Leroy missed some of the words. Lipreading at that stage in Leroy's life was difficult.

When his father talked, the words seemed to fly around the room. Catherine explained again to Leroy that he and his father would fly around, and when they landed he would be able to hear again. Leroy saw the joy in his father and mother's faces.

Leroy couldn't wait. The days seemed to draw out into weeks. At age seven, Leroy had never been up in an airplane. When the day finally came, Leroy and his father went to the airport. Peter carried Leroy because he had not yet regained full strength in his legs. The pilot escorted them to a small airplane. Peter picked up Leroy and placed him in the back seat of the plane, then climbed in beside his son. The pilot cranked up the propeller, and it turned clockwise slowly, picking up momentum. Leroy peered out the window in wonder at this machine. His father put his arm around his shoulder and smiled broadly, confident his son would regain his hearing. This was an important day.

The airplane taxied down the runway, passing grass-lands around it. Leroy saw some seabirds float by the airplane, brown pelicans heading to the Gulf to fish. The airplane made its ascent into the white clouds. The sky was bright blue. Large, puffy white clouds punctuated the horizon. The airplane flew farther over the Gulf. Leroy watched shrimp boats lined up to go into port. From that height, the shrimp boats in the Gulf looked like toys.

The pilot kept going higher and higher then did a strange maneuver. He made a fast nosedive toward the Gulf like a brown pelican plunging for fish. Leroy was afraid. Were they going to crash? But then he felt a strange tingling in his ear. His ears popped with the change in air pressure from high in the sky to low. He held onto the side of the plane and felt the vibrations of the engine. With the tingling in his ear, the pop in the air pressure and the vibrations on the side of the plane, Leroy thought he could hear. He yelled out to his father, "I can hear! I can hear!" His father was so excited he hugged his son and cried tears of joy.

The pilot made a quick ascent again up into the blue skies. Then he pointed the airplane's nose into a straight, vertical descent, down. Then again, and again, he repeated the ascents and descents. Leroy and his father became dizzy—Leroy's ears were popping and tickling. His hands were stuck on the side of the plane feeling the vibrations. He felt he was hearing again.

But when the plane landed, the tingling and popping which gave life to his ears disappeared. Leroy was still deaf, just as he was before he went up in the plane. Leroy could see the disappointment on his father's face when he told him that he still could not hear. His father said he should not worry. He and Leroy would try it again and again. Peter thought maybe he just needed more opportunities in the air to become hearing again. When Leroy and Peter returned home, Catherine was disappointed as well. But she, like Peter, refused to give up hope for their son to regain his hearing.

Throughout his life, Leroy repeated these aviation excursions to recapture the tingling and popping in his ears. Newspaper reporters noted that he frequently flew in airplanes with the "belief that the high altitude would help him regain his hearing." One reporter from *The San*

Antonio Light said of these airplane rides: "Lt. G. H. H. McHenry, an army airman, is taking Leroy Colombo, a deaf-mute on daily flights. Upon reaching an altitude of 11,000 feet, Lt. McHenry heads his plane straight down for each treatment and drops like a plummet 7,000 to 8,000 feet. Colombo reported that he can hear loud noises while the plane is diving and it is hoped eventually to restore his hearing completely."

In later years, a friend and schoolmate at the Texas School for the Deaf, Fred Mesa "Dummy" Mahan, a Deaf middleweight boxer, took such "curative" airplane rides. In adulthood, Mahan perished in an airplane crash, thus becoming a victim of the bogus cure.

Peter and Catherine were frustrated. They were weary from denial but not ready to release it. Nothing worked, yet they hoped that once Leroy got into school, their lives would quiet down and everything would be all right, back to normal, like it was before. That night in the family rosary, Peter and Catherine bowed their heads and prayed for a miracle for their son to regain his hearing. Maybe he would grow out of his deafness and become a hearing person again.

3

Frustration

Your tale, sir, would cure deafness.
The Tempest, William Shakespeare

Before his illness, Leroy had started first grade at Sam Houston Elementary School. Seated alongside his classmates, he learned to sound out his letters and read simple words. He made paintings of flowers, birds, and the beach. He brought these paintings home, and his mother pasted them on the kitchen wall. Leroy sang songs he learned at school with his mother. During that period of his life, he was not well, and he missed much school staying home in bed.

For months while he recovered from meningitis, Leroy was unable to walk. He tired quickly. In the mornings his mother helped him dress. He regained strength enough to walk to the kitchen for breakfast, but had to take rests even for that short distance.

One day Nick and Cinto schemed to take their brother out for fresh air. They knew their mother would disapprove. When she was busy in the kitchen, they carried Leroy out the front door and around to the back alleys of their neighborhood. These alleys were paved with white and gray broken oyster shells that formed a rocky pavement. The brothers gently propped Leroy on his feet. At first Leroy stumbled on the rough shells and fell on his backside. The brothers laughed. Leroy gritted his teeth, brushed off his trousers and stood back up, grinning. He took a step but fell again. The brothers continued to pick up Leroy and help him walk. After an hour of practice, they stopped. Leroy was hot and sweaty. Nick suggested they go to the beach and cool off in the surf.

Then the brothers carried Leroy on their shoulders to the beach. They held onto their brother, making a seat with their arms and carrying him into the waves. The threesome floated on their backs, holding hands. "Kick," the brothers told Leroy, "Kick those legs as hard as you can." Leroy kicked and kicked but still his legs moved only slightly.

While he could not stand on the sand without the support of his brothers' arms, in the water he felt free of his paralysis. He moved his upper body and made strong strokes into the waves; he was delighted to be back in the warm Gulf again. The months of pain and discomfort fell briefly from his memory, and he knew he had returned to his element.

The Gulf waters and sandy shores, though sometimes plagued by destructive hurricanes, had a narcotic effect on Leroy that would sustain him for the rest of his life. The beach would one day feel like his home whether he slept in cars or concession stands. The Gulf waters would become a stage where he could show the world that he was a competent swimmer, seawater racer, and lifeguard. The beach was his preacher's pulpit where he scolded errant flocks of swimmers and reminded them to stay away from the dangerous groins and avoid swimming out too deep. It was his classroom where he would teach children how to swim. And as it was his home and classroom, he worked to keep the beach safe, kicking off swimmers who were horsing around.

Every day, Nick and Cinto took Leroy for walking trips in the alleyways lined with the coarse oyster shells and for daily swims, pushing him to do more. But at first, Catherine, Peter, and his uncles did not approve. They feared for the boy's safety, Leroy explained later in his interview with Dr. Marquette.

Neither Leroy's paralysis nor his deafness could keep him restrained. With his brothers' help, he sneaked off to the beach against his parents' wishes. To Leroy, the over-protection and concern placed him in a prison from which he struggled to escape. When their mother found out, the boys explained to her that Leroy was not in any danger. "Just watch out for your brother," Catherine admonished.

This was an order that Cinto and Nick would follow for the remainder of their lives, especially Nick. Because of the nature of meningitis, which often causes a subsiding paralysis, Leroy's legs became stronger and stronger, a process augmented by his exercise in the fresh air and vigorous swims.

Many years later, a reporter from *The Galveston Daily News* gave his own interpretation of Leroy's rehabilitation: "When he was a little fellow, he had an illness that caused paralysis and he couldn't hear or talk anymore. The doctor said he would be paralyzed for the rest of his life, his sister-in-law said. But his brothers, they would put his arms around his neck and run up and down the alley in back of the house until his feet would be scarred. To get him to move his legs, they would go out on the beach and swim with him to build them up."

The summer after his first grade came to an end, it was time for Leroy to return to school. His stamina had improved. He was walking and wanted to join his brothers and sisters at school.

But when Leroy returned to his neighborhood schoo, the next year, he felt strange. He walked into the second grade classroom amid all the chatting children, and he still could not hear them. It was if he were in a soundproof room. He stared at all the moving mouths around him. His teacher recognized him and put her arm around him. She gestured for him to sit in the front row so he could see her lips.

Catherine and Peter had made numerous trips to the school before Leroy's first day so they could describe what their son needed. The teachers and staff worked hard to accommodate Leroy. They knew the Colombo family, and while they knew nothing of serving deaf children in the schools, they were determined to do the best they could.

At first, the teacher and the students showered Leroy with attention. They worked at speaking slowly and making sure that Leroy followed conversations directed to him. But some of his classmates responded with fright, and his deaf voice sounded like a foghorn. Leroy felt their fear and their eyes on his back. But slowly the children forgot about Leroy and were immersed in writing, drawing, talking, playing, and teasing each other.

When the teacher and the students returned to their routines, Leroy felt a sense of relief. The activities in his classes—lining up in the school yard, putting away belongings, finding classrooms, opening books, retrieving pencils dropped and rolling on the floor—filled his days at school with a comforting routine as it did for the other children. In some ways Leroy felt no different from his classmates.

However, Leroy's contentedness at school gradually turned to misery. He had to rely on his visual memory and lipreading skills to follow what was happening in the classroom, and this was both frustrating and fatiguing.

Watching a teacher's lips all day would be tiring for any seven year-old boy. Leroy's teacher sometimes forgot his needs as she turned her back to write on the blackboard even while talking to give the children instructions. Leroy missed all such explanations. He could see movements of the children around him, grabbing their pencils, taking out paper or switching activities, and he scrambled to mimic them. He often felt confused.

It wasn't possible for him to follow the conversations of the children behind him as they answered the teacher's requests. To make matters worse, the other children snickered at Leroy when he lost his place in round-robin reading. And when music time came, Leroy felt even more humiliated.

As the teacher played the piano and the other

children sang along, Leroy sang off key because he could not hear himself. He could see the girls and boys laughing, and blushed. One boy in the back of the room mocked Leroy's voice, and the children laughed with more vigor, something not lost on Leroy. He hid his red face in his arm.

One day, as Leroy drew a seagull flying over the beach, he failed to notice everyone leaving the room because of the fire alarm bell. The teacher and students had forgotten to tap Leroy on the shoulder as they usually did to let him know about a fire drill. When Leroy finally looked up from his drawing, he was stunned to discover that he sat alone in the room. Where were his teachers and classmates? He looked out the window and saw students from other classes lined up in the play yard, so he ran outside to find his teacher and his class. When the boys and girls in the schoolyard saw Leroy running to them, they all laughed. The teacher motioned the children to shush and gently brought Leroy over to his classmates. She leaned down and apologized to the boy. Leroy wanted to be invisible. He blushed a deep red and tucked his face into his shirt.

It was another day and another humiliation for a deaf boy living in a hearing world.

While classes were usually tolerable, especially when the teacher allowed him to draw after he finished his work, the recesses were unbearable. Outside, two rowdy bullies got Leroy between them and threw pebbles and seashells. Leroy pushed one boy, and a punching match started. Outnumbered and overpowered, Leroy fell to the ground with two big boys on top of him, one pulling his hair and punching him in the nose and the other one swinging fists into Leroy's stomach.

Nick and Cinto saw the squabble from across the playground and hurried over to help Leroy. They yelled at the boys and told them to leave Leroy alone. Leroy sobbed as he sat on the ground, his clothes dirty and his nose bleeding.

Such fights became frequent, and the teachers felt frustrated by having to break up so many fights in the schoolyard, fights that always involved the Colombo boys. Nick, Cinto and Leroy were secretly proud of how they could blacken eyes and bloody noses before the teachers could stop the fights. But inside, Leroy felt much pain. He was tired of the fighting and tired of not understanding what was going on around him.

In May 1913 the island flowers bloomed with red, yellow, and pink hibiscus, and the palm trees greened into spring. Oleanders lined the streets with white and pink blossoms. Brown pelicans hatched their babies and made extra trips to the Gulf for fish. Seagulls congregated on the beach, chasing sandpipers and eating sand crabs.

Leroy still went for frequent swims with Cinto and Nick. While school was difficult, the home front was easier for Leroy, especially those warm spring afternoons of freedom and bliss splashing in the warming waters. Then news came that sent the family reeling.

Catherine showed up at school one afternoon, her face lined with concern and worry. She summoned the children home as she said she had to go to the hospital. She talked slowly to the children, telling them that their father had been at work at the restaurant but had been rushed by ambulance to St. Mary's Hospital. She did not know what was wrong but had to go immediately to the hospital. The older girls were to take care of the house, as children were not allowed in the hospital. She shook her finger at the boys, warning them to behave and help their sisters. She then gave them each a kiss on the forehead.

Catherine came home that night weary to the bone. She slept, then was off to the hospital the next day. This went on for a week. She explained to the children that their father had suffered a heart attack and that the doctors were trying to save him.

Several days later, Catherine came home. The children were playing quietly on the porch. Catherine gathered her eight children around her, and she burst into tears. Their father had died of another heart attack while in the hospital. The nurses and doctors could not save him. The children felt numb at the news. Leroy was seven years old.

In the next few days, the children attended the wake and rosary service and the funeral mass. Leroy walked up to his father's open casket. His father did not look the same. Where was his tan? Where were his brown sparkly eyes? Leroy could not recognize the waxen face with its funeral home makeup. Leroy smelled a sweet-sickly odor of funeral lilies surrounding his father in the satin-lined casket.

The next day was the funeral mass in a church filled with Leroy's extended Italian family, men and women who worked with Peter at the restaurant, and many of the families in the neighborhood. Again Leroy felt left out. Lost in their own grief, his brothers and sisters would not tell him what was going on.

Left out of the words swirling around him and miserably alone during this painful time, Leroy's imagination ignited. He looked at the closed casket in front of the altar and imagined that the brown box had a secret air pocket that would allow his father to breathe. His father gently opened up the casket from the inside, sat up and waved to Leroy, then told Catherine and all the children that the funeral was a big mistake. Peter climbed out of the casket, and the family walked home.

Lost in this sweet reverie, Leroy stared blankly ahead of him. Then Nick elbowed Leroy in the ribs. Nick told Leroy that it was time to eat and to follow him. Outside in the churchyard, a feast had been prepared by the parishioners.

Friends and family shared stories and memories Leroy could not understand. He was isolated from the rituals that brought relief to others in mourning.

Leroy's father was only 51 years old when he died. He left behind his 40-year-old wife, eight young children, a large debt, and no life insurance policy. Catherine, a proud and strong woman, would raise her children as a single mother and live until 1944. When she died she was 71 years old and Leroy was 38.

Peter's death was an unexpected emotional and financial blow, bringing dramatic changes to the family. Nick, Leroy's eldest brother, quit school at age 10 so he could be the family provider. He worked for Western

Union, riding around the island on his bicycle delivering telegrams. Nick continued this role as "father" even when Leroy reached adulthood. When times were hard on Leroy and he needed extra cash, he often went to Nick's office or the back door of his home to ask for money. Years later, Nick's son Russ remarked in an interview that his father "never had a childhood."

Nick felt resentment at having to take care of his family, though he struggled not to show it. He gave up his childhood for his mother, brothers and sisters. Since he was the oldest son, many people expected him to take on the caretaker role vacated by his father's death.

The summer of 1913 was difficult for the Colombo family. The absence of Peter struck a sad note in the day-to-day goings on. In spite of it all, Leroy continued to swim at the beach every day, and Catherine continued to be busy with the younger children and could not supervise the older children. As a single mother so preoccupied with her own grief but unable to take time from her daily duties to take care of her own needs, she was always fatigued. The boys spent hours at the beach, and during the evenings they roamed the neighborhood streets playing tag and ball.

During the following two years, Leroy continued going to public school, but it was not a happy time. He could not keep up with the work, but his teachers felt sorry for the deaf, fatherless boy, so they passed him into the next grade, then into the next grade. The playground battles never ceased, and Leroy, Nick, and Cinto wore perpetual black eyes, as did the bullies.

Catherine was at a crossroads. Exhausted and confused, she was particularly concerned about Leroy. School was not working for him. It pained her to see him come home, depressed and lonely. She noticed him isolating himself more and more. Without anyone to talk to and with limited resources for her children—especially Leroy—she felt utterly lost.

4
Beginnings at TSD (1915-1918)

Sit still and hear the last of our sea-sorrow.
The Tempest, William Shakespeare

Catherine had little time to focus on her deaf son. Her time was spent cooking, washing clothes, and cleaning the house. Her older daughters and son became "child parents" who took care of the younger babies. There was no time in this emotionally chaotic Colombo home for negotiating or sharing feelings.

But still, Leroy's plight weighed heavily on his mother's mind. Catherine felt Leroy's pain. After two years, at age nine, he was failing in school. The teachers had decided not to keep passing him as they did in the earlier grades. The thinking then was that Leroy might catch up on his own. When teachers saw he was not catching up, they decided against passing him to another grade.

Leroy was like a fish out of water in the public school, and Catherine felt she had no options. She couldn't home school Leroy as there were still babies to take care of at home. Nor could she afford a private tutor to teach him at home.

Leroy's escape was daily swims with his brothers. In the Gulf, he felt free and forgot about his hearing. But at home, it was becoming increasingly stressful. His mother and brothers and sisters could sometimes understand his deaf speech because they were used to him. But sometimes they forgot and called Leroy from another room, then became angry when he didn't answer. Leroy felt frustrated too.

His response to his deafness and isolation resulted in feelings of anger, frustration and sadness, in not being able to communicate with those around him; this was hardly unique to Leroy Colombo. Dr. McCay Vernon, Dr. Irene Leigh and other psychologists have documented many cases of people responding thus to the onset of deafness.

Leroy was prone to big, explosive fits of anger that frightened his family, except for Nick and Cinto. They could wrestle Leroy to the ground and calm him. In his attempts to express his feelings, Leroy increasingly relied on physical actions because those around him weren't equipped to communicate with him in the ways he needed.

One sunny afternoon, Catherine decided she would talk to her brother, San Jacinto (also called Cinto) Gaido, a businessman on the island well known for financial and political acumen. He figured he would help her know what to do with her deaf son, how to help him get through the trauma he was experiencing at school and at home.

After quieting the children and instructing the older girls to take charge, Catherine took off her apron, put on a fresh dress, swiped lipstick lightly across her lips and grabbed her purse, checking for coins. She took a streetcar to the street across from Cinto's seafood café on Murdock's pier.

Catherine had a special relationship with Cinto. By raising him like a son when their mother died, she had kept him from having to live in an orphanage. Quite a bit older than Cinto, Catherine nevertheless relied on him for advice in financial matters.

Cinto welcomed his older sister and gestured to her to follow him to a quiet area in the back of the café. He ordered two coffees and two Italian cream cakes, a dessert he knew his sister had loved since childhood. Catherine took out her handkerchief and cried.

"Leroy?" he asked. She nodded and shared with her brother some of the challenges he had faced at school and at home. Cinto listened with concern and told her about a special school in Austin for deaf children like Leroy. He had passed the school numerous times when he was on business in Austin buying supplies for his restaurant. There, Cinto explained, Leroy could learn to read and write and be with boys and girls who were like him.

At first, Catherine was reluctant. Leroy was only nine years old. She could not bear to send him away where she would not be able to comfort him when he was sad or kiss him and tuck him in at night. San Jacinto gently pressed the idea, talking about how the school would help Leroy, explaining that living there would be in the boy's best interest. She nodded and sobbed into her handkerchief. What would the neighbors think, she asked herself, about sending Leroy away at such a tender age?

In spite of her misgivings, Catherine knew Cinto was

right. She finished her coffee and dessert and headed home.

In the first part of the summer, shortly after shool ended for the year, she took Leroy aside and explained to him that she and Uncle Cinto had exciting news to share with him. They had found him a new school where he would learn many new things. He would live at the school, and his teachers would teach him how to speak again.

Leroy wanted none of this new plan. He burst into tears and said he did not want to leave home but to stay with his brothers and sisters. He promised he would behave and not get into so many fights. Catherine assured him that his fighting was not the reason that he should leave home. The problem was, she explained, that the school in Galveston was not working out. He needed a special school where there were boys and girls just like him. As the summer months passed, Leroy seemed less traumatized about the plans to move him to Austin.

The month of August rolled in. Catherine began gathering what she wanted Leroy to have when he moved to the new school. One evening in mid-August, Catherine stood over Leroy's large metal and leather trunk, opened wide in Leroy's bedroom. Cinto and Nick and his sisters were all helping Leroy pack. Catherine folded several pairs of knickers and shirts and placed them neatly in the corner of the trunk. She added towels and bars of soap. Leroy folded up two bathing suits and placed them on top. He wondered if the school had a beach where he could swim. He would miss swimming in the Gulf with Cinto and Nick. Finally, on top, Catherine placed a framed picture of Leroy and his brothers and sisters with their father, Peter.

The next morning Catherine and Leroy took the streetcar to the train station after saying goodbye to the rest of the family. Leroy's brothers and sisters stood in the front yard and waved.

Catherine and Leroy boarded the train and found a seat near the window. As the train rambled north and west, they watched the countryside seem to zip by in its turning from the familiar landscape of subtropical Galveston to pasture lands, then to dry, desert-like landscape with scrubby, low-lying bushes on the outskirts of Austin. It took the train all day to make the 213 mile trip.

Leroy fell asleep against his mother. An arm around him, Catherine looked down at her young, innocent son and wondered if she had made the right decision.

When the train stopped in Austin, they had Leroy's trunk carried to the streetcar, and together they rode across town, up South Congress Avenue and over the bridge. At the school's front entrance gate they read the sign: "Texas Asylum for the Deaf and Dumb." They entered the campus through iron gates and walked until they came to the main building, a large one that had two tall towers.

As they entered the building, a stern, portly woman in a black dress and white apron greeted them. She was the matron and was expecting them, as Catherine had written a letter informing the school when she and her son would arrive. The matron explained that Superintendent Urbantke was in a meeting but would be with them shortly. She described how the Texas School, called TSD, had more than 400 students from all over Texas. The matron did not use sign language, as she knew that neither Leroy nor his mother knew it. They sat in the waiting room.

In a short time, Mr. Urbantke stepped out of his office. Sharon Hovinga and Franna Camenisch in their history of the Texas School for the Deaf, Mr. Gus C. Urbantke was a dark, stocky man of German descent. He had taught for a while in Houston then had become a college professor for Blinn College where he taught for 24 years before taking the superintendent position. He had also been president of the Brenham Public School Board.

Mr. Urbantke welcomed Leroy and his mother to campus. He assured the concerned mother that he and his teachers and staff at TSD would take care of Leroy. Her son would join 400 other students who were currently on the campus. There would be lots of opportunity for Leroy as TSD had a variety of courses and vocational opportun-ities from which he could choose.

The matron then took Leroy and his mother to a nearby table where she opened a large, leather-bound enrollment book and handed Catherine a fountain pen. With a trembling hand she signed her name, enrolling her son into the Texas Asylum for the Deaf and Dumb on August 23, 1915.

The enrollment document Catherine signed is dis-played today in the Heritage House Museum at the Texas School for the Deaf. Leroy was nine at the time; he turned ten that December.

After a quick tour of the classrooms, the dormitory and playground, Catherine said goodbye to her son. Both mother and son cried as she walked out the gate to catch a streetcar to the train station. Catherine shed more tears on the train ride home, and wondered again if she had made the right decision. She knew Leroy's brothers and sisters would be waiting for her at home and wondering how Leroy liked his new school.

Leroy's first night in the dormitory at the Primary Oral Building seemed tolerable enough, in part because of his fatigue after the long train trip to Austin from Galveston. He was used to sharing a room with his brothers so, in some ways, sleeping in a dorm was like sleeping at home. He felt intimidated the first morning in the dining room where the children ate breakfast. Intrigued by the flying fingers and hands around him, he asked the dorm supervisor to teach him some signs.

After breakfast, the dorm supervisor directed Leroy to return to his room. He mimicked the other boys who made their beds then went to the bathroom to brush their teeth. Leroy followed the children to a classroom when it was time for study. For the first few weeks, until he learned some sign language, he followed the boys around the school and copied what they did.

One boy came over to Leroy and began signing to him rapidly. Leroy shook his head and raised his arms. The boys smiled then slowed down his signing. Then he began instructing Leroy in sign. This is the sign for "no." This is the sign for "yes." This is the sign for "good morning." The boy modeled the signs for Leroy, and he copied them. This is the sign for "pea brain." The other boys who assembled around the new boy laughed. One boy even taught Leroy some vulgar signs for sex and for excrement but warned Leroy not to use them around adults or he would be in trouble.

Soon Leroy had a circle of Deaf friends who helped him learn sign language whenever he asked. He gradually picked up sign on the playground, in the dining room, and in the dormitory at night. At first, he felt out of place, but he gradually felt more comfortable. He could see what people were talking about and as soon as his sign language abilities increased, he felt more a part of the Deaf world.

According to historians Hovinga and Camenisch, the students' school routine during Leroy's time began early in the morning in the primary oral classroom with other boys and girls who were ages nine and ten. The play areas, separated for boys and girls, were divided by the dining hall on the first floor. The classrooms were on the second floor, and the third floor was reserved for separate boys' and girls' dormitories.

That first morning, Leroy sat in a classroom with eight other children behind a wooden table that made an "L" shape so every child could see each other's lips. This class was called an "oral class," and sign language was not permitted. Like him, the children in this class had speech before they became deaf from diseases in early childhood. The children in the oral class would also be taught fingerspelling on the hand. They were taught to speak and lipread the words from the motions of the tongue, lips, and mouth. They then added fingerspelling to spell out words they could not pronounce very well.

The first word Leroy learned to fingerspell was his first name. He fingerspelled L-E-R-O-Y and showed his

Deaf friends. Next he learned to spell where he was born and the names of his brothers and sisters. When he got back to the dorm, he showed his roommates what he had learned. Leroy's schoolmates gave him a name sign, a custom in many Deaf communities. Leroy's name sign was made with the letter "C" formed by cupping the fingers and thumb into a "C" shape with the right hand, then the right hand is placed on the left side of the forehead. Leroy kept this name sign for the rest of his life.

When he returned home, Leroy couldn't wait to teach his mother and siblings how to fingerspell. But he was discouraged because after they learned the basics of it, no one in the family used it much with him. In an interview as an adult Leroy said, "I wish my mother learned the finger language."

But at TSD outside of class in the play area and in the dormitories, the children's fingers flew, not in fingerspelling but with sign language. The children seldom used speech unless a hearing teacher was around and it was demanded. They all much preferred to use sign language because it was easier and more fluid and came more naturally than the strain and struggle of speech. To Leroy, all of this signing initially looked like a flurry of movement, much like the wind-swept palm trees on Galveston Island: pretty but essentially meaningless. Over time, though, he was able to decipher the motions and attach meaning to them, thus gaining a new language.

In the classroom, signing was not permitted. Blackboards covered two sides of the room behind the seated children, blackboards that contained much writing.

Students practiced writing words on the blackboard daily to supplement and support their speech lessons. A two-foot by two-foot mirror hung on the blackboard so the children could look at their mouth, lip, and tongue movements as they practiced correct locution, something modeled by the teacher. White chalk and erasers covered the ledge under the blackboard. A toy doll sat on an empty chair just waiting for the girls to play. Photographs of the room taken during the era when Leroy Colombo attended the school showed balls and bats for the boys in the corner of the room. The classroom was a happy place, and the teacher made sure the children had fun and took frequent breaks. She knew that Deaf children's eyes tire easily and that they needed to move around and change activities so they would not become sleepy or bored.

The girls wore navy dresses, and the boys wore khaki knickerbockers, white shirts, and ties. Leroy's mother had left money so he could buy his uniforms at TSD.

The children studied speech, reading, writing, and mathematics in the morning class. As did the others, Leroy practiced writing letters and words using chalk and a slate board, and practiced forming sounds using the mirror.

One morning the teacher handed him a small mirror and motioned for him to copy her as she showed him how to form speech sounds. She placed a wooden stick in Leroy's mouth and took his hand and placed it on his throat. Leroy could feel the vibrations and match these tactile sensations to the forming of sounds on the lips. It was tedious work.

But Leroy was a good speech student because he had

heard words for the first six years of his life. The other boys and girls who lost their hearing at birth or before age three had a more difficult time learning to talk. Leroy was frequently called to the front of the classroom to demonstrate his speech for visitors. At age ten, he enjoyed being center stage. Sometimes he laughed and mimicked someone. He enjoyed performing for an audience, a personality trait he developed in boyhood and kept throughout his lifetime. Leroy was a crowd pleaser, and he liked to make people laugh. Acting silly or making a joke helped him put hearing people at ease when they became uncomfortable attempting to communicate with him.

When Christmas came that first year, Leroy stayed at school during the holidays like other Deaf children. A train ticket home was too expensive for the families of most children. Leroy missed his family, but he had made many new friends at TSD, and after three months of practice, his sign language skills had improved, so he was not bored at school—plus there was always plenty to do.

For Christmas older children had decorated the chapel, the classrooms, and the dormitories with Spanish moss, cedar, laurel and colorful autumn leaves, giving the school a festive appearance. Some of the children put on a school play to celebrate the holidays. All students assembled in a large room, and the younger children watched with fascination as the older students acted out the story of Christmas. All those on stage used sign language so the children could understand what was happening in the story. There was even a baby Jesus, the infant child of one of the teachers who generously allowed her baby to pose in the manager. She stood nearby, dressed in Mary's costume to take care of the baby.

Leroy sat in the front row and cheered with his friends when the play ended and the lights went back on. After the play, the children were treated to yellow taffy and bags of nuts. On another day during Christmas break, the children wrote letters to Santa. Hovinga and Camenisch quote a letter by one boy who wrote to Santa: "Please bring me lots of toys to play with…I am a very good boy. I do not fight. I do not sign. I am not a crybaby. Now please bring me some toys."

On the playground Leroy learned the pecking order among the boys. The older ones bossed the younger boys when choosing sides for games. Leroy was pushed a few times, but he was able to defend himself. He some-times missed the protection of Cinto and Nick, but not all of the boys at the school were bullies.

Some taught Leroy more signs and shared candies and cookies they received from home. He especially liked the dorm parents who often taught him more signs or helped him with his chores and homework. Some of the men seemed like fathers to him. Leroy missed his father, and he sometimes imagined that a favorite dorm parent was his father, brought back to life.

Aside from his studies, Leroy watched silent movies in the auditorium. With his classmates, he often took the streetcar to go to Austin where he could see more movies and buy ice cream.

One afternoon, Leroy and his buddies took the street-car from TSD to Bull Creek for an afternoon of swimming, a place, according to Camenisch, that was popular for Deaf students to swim. Next to Bull Creek was a resort with a Ferris wheel, and the boys couldn't wait to ride it in the afternoon after their swim.

They changed into their suits in the wooden bathhouses. There was a diving board at the pool and as they watched, a lady dove 50 feet into the pool. Leroy, awed by this circus-like performance, dreamed that someday he would be a diver. All afternoon the boys practiced their diving into the pool doing jackknives, flips, and back dives.

That afternoon they changed back into their clothes and went to the fair where they rode the Ferris wheel long into the evening. The big wheel went around the sky, and the boys looked at the stars. They ate cotton candy and hot dogs, drank lemonade and played games until they had to return to school.

Leroy's life at TSD was enriched by activities and friends, and he busied himself with schoolwork. Before long he became a good signer. He developed a pride in his school, just as the other boys and girls did. He felt accepted and took joy in being able to understand the conversations around him. Surrounded by caring adults who had his best interests at heart, the state school became a real home for Leroy. At the school he met adults who would become surrogate mothers and fathers. His Deaf friends would later follow his athletic races in the Deaf periodicals, and many traveled to his beach when he was a lifeguard to picnic and visit with him.

At home in Galveston, Catherine had scraped up enough money to pay for Leroy's train ticket from Austin to Galveston so he could come home for the summer. Leroy had written frequent letters home saying he loved TSD and had made lots of friends. His report cards showed he was learning to read and write, and Catherine was pleased that she had found a school for Leroy where he was doing well.

Catherine had found some stability in her life, especially with Nick bringing in a regular paycheck from his work at Western Union, and she picked up some money doing sewing and laundry for families in the neighborhood. The older girls were babysitting, too, and the money they earned helped the family.

Leroy couldn't wait to get on the train and get home. He missed his mother, brothers and sisters, though he felt a bit sad to leave the school because he knew that back home in Galveston, no one would use sign language with him, and he feared being left out. But he did not dwell on such thoughts, for his mind was on more important things: swimming in the Gulf, playing horseshoes on the beach with his brothers.

Later in the summer he developed the habit of following the lifeguards around and copying their swimming and exercise routines.

The ride to the train station by streetcar and then by train to his home seemed to take an eternity for the boy. But finally he arrived in Galveston where his mother met him at the train station.

5
First Save

...Leads me, lures me, calls me
To salt green tossing sea:
A road without earth's road-dust
Is the right road for me.

"Roadways," John Masefield

Leroy settled into his new life at TSD. He made Deaf friends and formed close relationships with his teachers and dorm parents. Alongside his Deaf peers he studied, played and developed new interests including swimming in the cold, spring-fed swimming areas in Austin. He watched silent movies in the school auditorium. On the school fields, he played baseball and football. His signed language developed rapidly, and in the classroom he learned reading, writing, and mathematics. Leroy progressed through the elementary grades without the difficulty and frustration he endured at the Sam Houston Elementary School in Galveston.

TSD gave Leroy a center and a stability because he

was surrounded by boys and girls and adults who could communicate with him on a daily basis.

But Leroy also loved coming home to see his mother and brothers and sisters. He especially wanted to swim in the Gulf with his brothers and older lifeguards. One summer in 1918 was particularly eventful.

He was 12 and a half years old, and he was changing from boyhood to adolescence. It was typically hot and humid on Galveston Island, and tourists, like colonies of white egrets, flocked by the hundreds to the beaches.

In Jodi Wright-Gidley and Jennifer Marines' book *A City on Stilts* the authors call Galveston beaches "the playground of Texas." Tourists and locals alike grabbed towels and suits and headed to the sandy shore. They perched on chairs under umbrellas and stretched out on the sand to sun, and many went swimming. As Texans became more affluent and cars more plentiful, many people eyed Galveston as a fun summer driving destination.

Tourists came not only to enjoy the water and the cool Gulf breezes, but to experience the quaintness of Galveston Island. Pink and white oleanders bordered the streets, and palm tree fronds cut through the air like fans. In the morning, the beachfront erupted with black-and-white-striped umbrellas popping open along the sandy shore. Children fed the seagulls their leftover snacks and ran in and out of the surf, ignoring their parents behind them yelling, "Don't get wet yet, you don't have your suit on!"

The Colombo boys spent the morning splashing and body surfing in the warm waves. They raced in the water and tumbled onto the shore to rest before running back into the churning surf. They frequently lay on the sand face up then turned over to dry in the sun. By summer's end, Leroy's skin had become bronze.

The Colombo boys became friends with the volunteer lifeguards, and the boys trained with them by swimming long laps up and down the Gulf. They jogged with the men and joined them in their morning exercises on the beach. The boys looked up to the volunteer lifeguards and wanted to be just like them when they grew up.

One July afternoon, Leroy and his brothers were in their usual spot at the beach. Nick and Cinto had dared each other to a race down the beach and left Leroy sunning by himself, lost in an afternoon daydream.

Leroy sat up abruptly, for a lone seagull had pooped on his outstretched leg. He made the sign for *shit*, then he took a handful of sand and rubbed the white runny blob from his leg and grimaced in disgust. The seagull cawed and flew away.

While sitting upright, Leroy spotted a swimmer flailing in the water. He recognized at once that the swimmer was in trouble. From watching lifeguards at work, Leroy knew just what to do.

He kept his eyes on the boy who clung to the wooden groin. But the waves butted against the side of the wooden seawall and pushed him under water. Each time he came up distressed, thrashing his arms in a futile attempt to hang on to the groin. This was a drowning victim, and Leroy knew it. He looked up and down the beach, and seeing no lifeguards, he ran to the water and dove in. With practiced, even crawl strokes, he propelled himself through the water and out to the boy, all the while keeping his head out of the water to keep an eye on the distressed boy.

When Leroy reached him, the panicked boy, in trying to cling to Leroy, hit him hard on the side of his face. Leroy went under water and came back, aware of a pain in his left jaw. He swam behind the boy as Leroy had seen the lifeguards approach other drowning victims from behind. Leroy wrapped his arm around the boy's neck and pulled him from the pilings, and the exhausted boy stopped struggling. Holding the boy's head in a strong arm-lock, Leroy pulled him toward the shore. The boy was heavy, and it took all of Leroy's strength to pull him in.

Over his left shoulder, in his peripheral vision, Leroy saw a blue blob bouncing on the waves. The blue ball came toward him and the boy. Leroy knew this was no ball. It was a Portuguese man-of-war jellyfish with its long stinging tendrils swinging in the water. If those tendrils got them, the two of them might be paralyzed in the water and drown.

Leroy knew that swimmers, especially children, sometimes mistook a Portuguese man-of-war for a toy ball and became tangled in the animal's long tendrils. Such swimmers had to be rushed to a hospital to be treated for the dangerous stings.

Leroy stopped his forward motion and began to tread water. He let the jellyfish have the right of way, and the blue blob floated farther down the beach. By taking such a precaution, Leroy evaded the jellyfish and made it to the beach safely with the heavy boy in his grasp.

Safely on shore, the boy regained his breath and coughed up much salt water. A lifeguard who had spotted Leroy and the boy out in the deeper water knelt beside the boy and gave him a towel. He made sure the boy was all right and cautioned him not to swim near the groins, as there were rip currents there that could wear down even the strongest swimmer. The boy agreed and shook hands with Leroy. His worried mother rushed over to give him a scolding and a towel and escorted him back to their umbrella.

Cinto and Nick and several other seasoned lifeguards had witnessed Leroy's rescue as well as his maneuvers away from the man-of-war jellyfish. The lifeguards, wearing their standard uniforms—red swimsuits with white safari hats and metal whistles around their necks—approached Leroy and slapped him affectionately on his back. They congratulated him on his heroic save. Nick and Cinto beamed with pride. Secretly they felt envious that their deaf brother was getting all the attention.

Leroy's chest puffed out. He liked the praise from men he respected. He liked the power of being in con-trol when he rescued a drowning victim, and he knew that he wanted to be a lifeguard just like the men who stood around him.

For the remainder of the summer, Leroy continued to develop his swimming skills. He spent time with the older lifeguards who allowed Leroy, Nick, and Cinto to join them in their morning exercises of lap swimming in the Gulf. Leroy also spent time that summer studying tides and wave actions. Observing the Gulf and its changes, he watched the water as it changed colors from light green to brown and became turbulent with the currents.

When tourists stepped on the small balls of tar periodically floating to the beach, Leroy often showed them how to use turpentine to clean their feet.

Although still in their teens, Leroy, Cinto, and Nick were singled out by the experienced lifeguards. The men invited the Colombo brothers to join them on Sunday afternoons for a long-distance swim. The first few times they tried it, none of the boys could finish. But they practiced and practiced, for the boys' goal was to join the prestigious lifeguard club called the STC, or the Surf Toboggan Club, and thus have the honor of wearing the STC insignia on their tee shirts.

The STC would later be Leroy's training ground for his future life as a lifeguard. But he had to wait until he was older. The STC attracted the strongest swimmers on the beach, and Leroy, Nick, and Cinto were certainly eager to become part of this group.

The news of Leroy's dramatic rescue spread among the Galveston beach lifeguards, and it was more than anything else, the single event that propelled Leroy into a career as a lifeguard. He developed the necessary physical stamina, and he had the natural athletic ability. The summer of that first rescue he was learning much about the habits of the tricky Gulf waters. The months of summer ended too quickly to suit Leroy, and in September when he was back on the train to Austin, he felt sadness for leaving his family and the beach.

6
More TSD (1918-1922)

Here in this island we arrived, and here
Have I, thy schoolmaster, made me more profit
Than other princes can, that have more time
For vainer hours, and tutors not so careful.
The Tempest, William Shakespeare

It was September 1918. According to Texas School for the Deaf historians Hovinga and Camenisch, superintendent Urbantke led the school in major improvements on TSD campus. Anti-German feelings following World War I were prevalent all over the USA, and Austin was no exception. The TSD Board of Trustees decided to dismiss super-intendent Urbantke because of his German heritage and because someone accused him of "feeding sauerkraut to the pupils." The Deaf community did not agree with the Board's decision.

The next superintendant was Dr. Felix B. Shuford, a physician from Tyler, Texas who began his work in 1919 and left TSD in 1923. He was a man who did not know sign language and was a strict disciplinarian, a man who would not tolerate any behavior outside his stringent code of conduct. Just four days into his job, he recommended to the board that several students be expelled for disobedience and immoral behavior. Leroy was happy he was not among them.

Even though Mr. Shuford was a strict disciplinarian, according toHovinga and Camenisch, he had profound insight into the Deaf child's world and this included Leroy's situation. He was quoted by a reporter as saying, "Children come to us who did not know so much as their names, living in unrelieved isolation and darkness, no development afforded them, without companionship, even though surrounded by kin. No wonder the children come back here and they call this home! Here they have opportunity for expression and development. They are educated and trained to compete with the world, to render service in which there is the real joy of living, and that is all these girls and boys want—none of your pity, none of your tears, only a square deal!"

Despite the political shifts with superintendents changing, Leroy's life at school on the surface remained the same. He and the others enjoyed themselves on weekends and on holidays. While much of Leroy's day was spent in the classroom learning and studying, the era was the beginning of the Roaring Twenties, and there were many parties and plays at TSD. The girls in sewing classes made costumes for plays, and they dressed up as flappers for parties. The boys competed in sports on baseball and basketball teams. The school had "spirit."

During the warmer weather the boys and the girls went on picnics where they ate outside and went swimming. Many of these swimming holes were fed by springs and by the Colorado River, so Leroy experienced swimming in water much colder than in the warm Gulf of Mexico—experience that helped him build stamina and endurance, two traits that he would carry back to Galveston where he would win many saltwater sea races as a youth and young man.

A favorite pastime for Leroy and the boys and girls at TSD was movie night. One evening, Leroy lined up with the other boys and girls to go to the school auditorium where they watched silent movies from the movie picture machine. In prior years, the Texas legislature had appropriated $100 to the school to buy a silent movie machine, according to Hovinga and Camenisch, and using it remained a favorite pastime of the students and faculty.

One day Leroy was so excited that he could not sit still in class. His teacher gently reminded the children that if they broke any rules, they would join the other misbehaving boys and girls who sat in the principal's office and were not permitted to go to the movies.

During the comical movies, the actors made exaggerated facial expressions and wild body movements, like dancers and mimes, writes Dr. John Schuchman in *Hollywood Speaks: Deafness and the Film Industry*. Leroy and his classmates could not always read the few captions, but they did not need to. They laughed and laughed at the silly antics of the characters. The Deaf boys and girls kept their eyes glued to the movie screen.

Their favorite actors were Charlie Chaplin and his costar, Granville Redmond, who was deaf. The Deaf community felt great pride in Redmond's accomplishments, and to the children at TSD, Granville was very special, not only because he was deaf but because he made them laugh out loud. Many of the boys said they were going to Hollywood to become movie actors just like Granville.

On the movie night when the teacher had warned the boys not to misbehave, the students sat spellbound for two hours. They drank in the funny antics of Chaplin and Redmond, laughing at the crazy routines of the actors. When the boys and girls left the auditorium that evening, they walked back to the dorms imitating the funny walk of Chaplin. During the next days and weeks, they playacted the story plots in the hallways, dormitories, dining hall and even in chapel. The teachers hid their smiles. They could not reprimand children for enjoying playacting.

The days, then weeks, then months, then years passed quickly. Leroy grew into his teens with the support of his Deaf teachers and Deaf peers at school. But every June he could not wait to return to Galveston to his family and to the freedom of the Gulf. Then when each August came around, he was ready to return to the Austin school to be with his friends.

The Roaring Twenties blew into Austin with the force of a Gulf hurricane. This tumultuous time hit the high school department the hardest, for the high school kids were curious about cigarettes, alcohol, and the opposite gender. It was a carefree time and a challenging time to the more strict personalities that worked at schools and churches. Values were under question. The rules of society were frequently broken. And the young teens in the high school wanted to learn all about being a flapper, a dancer, a gambler, a drinker, and a smoker. And they wanted more opportunities to socialize with the opposite sex and to do so in less confining circumstances than those in school-sponsored dances on campus where the prim dorm matrons spied on them watching for infractions of rules. Many youths, churning with changing hormones, stayed up late at night to plan clandestine parties. Leroy was no different.

The days, weeks, months, and years passed quickly. Leroy grew into his teens at the school for the Deaf and the world of education was opened to him through American Sign Language. But every June, he could not wait to return home to Galveston to spend time with his family and time on the beach. He was popular with the older lifeguards, and this provided him with a male support system left vacant by the death of his father. But every August he was ready to return to Austin to school to be with his Deaf friends. Communication was so much easier in Austin because everyone knew sign language. Immersed in both the Deaf world at school and the hearing world at home and on the beach, Leroy made his way.

One dark, rainy night in 1922 when Leroy was 16, he and several of his classmates sneaked past the dorm supervisor who was immersed in his newspaper. Using a makeshift rope of bed sheets, the boys climbed out a dormitory window on the third floor and shimmied down a rusty drainpipe past the classroom windows on the first floor. Barefoot so as not to awaken the hearing watchman, they padded across the porch and down the stairs into the wet grass.

The boys tiptoed and headed quietly to the Heritage House, several buildings away from the main building. The rain came down softly, making mud puddles in the grass. But the boys did not care. It was warm enough to be barefooted. The boldest boy had previously worked out a deal where the laundry ladies would buy them cigarettes and beer and bring the contraband to the Heritage House late at night for a party. Leroy and the other boys chipped in a few dollars apiece.

At the Heritage House, it was dark except for the light of a few candles. One boy passed around cigarettes. Another boy passed the candle to light cigarettes. Another opened bottles of beer and passed them into eager hands. They toasted TSD and Superintendent Shuford. They toasted their parents, their winning basketball team, and their girlfriends. They even toasted President Warren Harding. One boy pulled a deck of cards from his pocket; others threw coins on the floor, and a fast-paced poker game started. When the young ladies behind the piles of dirty laundry saw the boys, they put their hands over their mouths and giggled and joined them. Smoke filled the room, and the candles began to flicker. Hours passed and the boys forgot about the time. Woozy with beer and lightheaded from cigarette smoke, some of the boys fell asleep on the piles of laundry. Two boys paired off with the laundry ladies and started necking.

At about 3 a.m., the dorm supervisor walked down

the hallway. He stopped at one bed and pulled back the covers. He found clothes stuffed under the covers to make it appear like the boy was sleeping. Six other boys had done likewise. He quickly summoned another watchman. The watchmen lit several gas lanterns, and glowing gaslights in hand, they searched the campus for the missing boys.

They searched the Heritage House and discovered the illicit party. The boys were drunk and sleepy, and Leroy was right in the middle of them. The laundry ladies had fled in embarrassment. The watchmen shook the boys' arms to wake them before scolding them using sign language, and the boys knew they were in deep trouble.

The boys only had a few hours to sleep before classes started. They were all hung over. Leroy had a terrible headache, but he had liked the taste of beer. It relaxed him and made him feel calm. He wanted to try it again.

Later, he would develop health problems from relying on beer and whiskey to relax him after his races or a busy day of lifeguarding. But that day he was only 16, and beer tasted just fine.

Later that afternoon, the boys tried to keep awake in class, but their heads kept dipping toward their desks. By then the teachers knew what had happened and felt sorry for the boys and let them sleep it off in class. But soon, as was expected, a messenger came to the classroom. The six boys were to go to Dr. Shuford's office.

Dr. Shuford made them wait in his office until a sign language interpreter came. "How dare you," he scolded, "bring cigarettes and liquor to this campus. I am ashamed of you!" He repeated himself over and over. The interpreter signed everything Dr. Shuford said: "Disobedience and immoral behavior will not be tolerated at this school." He droned on, his face turning an ugly red, and his bushy eyebrows arching in disdain. His mouth formed a deep frown.

One boy tried to make an excuse, explaining that they meant no harm but just wanted to playact what they had seen in the films.

But Dr. Shuford was not convinced. He called the boys delinquents, scoundrels, and scaliywags before telling them they needed to pack their bags and go home. Then Dr. Shuford uttered his last sentence as he slammed his fist on the desk: "You are expelled." Ironically, Mr. Shuford did not give Leroy and the boys the "square deal" he had told reporters that Deaf children need.

It was May 22, 1922, and Leroy was only 16 years old.

7

Seawater Racer

I think he will carry this island home in his pocket,
And give it to his son for an apple.
The Tempest, William Shakespeare

Leroy was crestfallen. He did not understand why the superintendent had responded so severely for such a harmless nighttime party. He loved TSD and hated to leave. Here his friends knew him by his name sign, a sign signaling respect. Every day at school, signs spilled from his hands, and his friends reciprocated by signing back conversations and stories, from early morning to late at night. They even signed in the bathrooms when the lights were out and they were supposed to be sleeping. The boys and girls laughed at Leroy's jokes, and he laughed at theirs.

At TSD, Leroy had formed a close friendship with a dorm father who was Deaf and who became a father-substitute to the confused and lonely teenager. He pitched Leroy and his classmates baseballs during those long Austin evenings outside the dorm when there was still sunlight. He sat beside Leroy and the other boys in the dorm, helping them with their homework. He took an interest in Leroy's progress at school and asked him about his love for swimming. For a lifetime, Leroy would miss his TSD father and silently slip into an emotional slump from which only winning races, accumulating trophies, saving lives and drinking alcohol could rescue him.

But he also had ambivalent feelings about the Deaf school. Life there could be confining. He missed the chaos of his home and the freedom of the beach and his long swims in the Gulf. At TSD, he always had to do what he was told. He couldn't sleep late, snack whenever he wanted, stay up late or fill his hours with daydreams. And then there was homework. His teachers were strict and demanding and took education seriously. Life on the beach was an enticing alternative.

He felt badly about the expulsion. He knew his mother would be disappointed, and he was humiliated to have to confront her after she got the news from the school, and he knew there would be a letter to his mother. On the ride home on the train, he looked out the window and wondered what lay ahead of him. He would have to face all his family.

Arriving home, Leroy was welcomed with open arms. His mother gently scolded him but then never brought up the subject again. He tumbled onto the rug with Nick and Cinto in a wrestling match. A lamp toppled to the floor and smashed into pieces. The boys stopped and looked up, expecting a scolding. But instead they saw their mother smiling. She was happy to have her son home. She quickly dropped her smile, reprimanded the boys, and sent them off to the beach.

Because he was 16, Texas law did not require Leroy to return to high school. He felt he did not need a diploma, so instead of worrying about school, he hung out at the house and helped with chores. Every afternoon he headed to the beach to visit with the lifeguards or take solitary walks.

On one of these walks on the beach, he burst into tears and cried uncontrollably for hours. TSD had been his home just as long as Galveston had been, and it was difficult to think that he likely wouldn't see any of his friends again. But then his tears and depression lifted when he looked out on the Gulf. Leroy's feelings of rejection from the expulsion began to wane. He felt a connection to the sea, the calm and topsy-turvy, churning Gulf that changed her moods often. The sunshine reflected from the foam-laced water, and the long, sandy shore lay before him. The Gulf filled his soul, his mind and his heart, and he knew this island was home.

After months of contentment at home, surprising news came in the mail. A letter arrived from the Deaf school, addressed to Mrs. Peter Colombo from Superintendent Thomas M. Scott. Catherine read the letter slowly aloud to Leroy. He and his five buddies were exonerated and invited back to school.

Superintendent Scott might be a gentler, more lenient man than the one who expelled Leroy, but it did not take long for Leroy to decide not to return to school. His family no doubt pointed out that it was foolhardy for a young Deaf youth to abandon his education given that jobs were scarce for hearing people and even more scarce for Deaf people. But Leroy was not persuaded. Perhaps if his father had lived, Peter would have insisted Leroy finish school. Maybe his mother did insist, and Leroy refused.

In the short time he had been out of school, Leroy tasted the thrill of lifesaving and sea racing. He was starting to win races in the Gulf, so he made the decision to stay home on Galveston Island instead of returning to the Deaf school. Galveston was just too exciting for Leroy, standing as he was on the cusp of adulthood. He enjoyed whiskey and the beer in the bars, dancing and gambling in the nightclubs, parties on the beach, and sea races where young women in bathing suits flocked around him.

Leroy and his brothers and friends had already sampled the nightlife in the bars and casinos. Though hot and humid, summer nights were filled with fun as the boys patrolled the bars and beaches with their friends. They liked it.

Leroy's memories of school life at TSD faded. But even though Leroy left the Deaf school in Austin, he continued his contacts with his Deaf classmates from the school and with other Deaf athletes in Texas. They would often come to Galveston, picnic on the beach and visit with Leroy according to Jerry Hassell in an interview. On nearly any sunny day, there was a flurry of hands using sign language on the beach. Leroy's friends filled him in on news in the Deaf world, so he felt again connected to TSD, his Deaf home.

His Deaf friends also came to watch Leroy compete in local races, and writers from Deaf periodicals frequently came to Galveston to watch his races and write about him in *The Silent Worker* and *The Deaf American*, two periodicals widely read in the Deaf community. On one special day, several deaf friends came to watch him race.

It was 1925 and Splash Day, the opening day of the beach, and Leroy stood on the pier with six other swimmers, all ready to race. The Galveston celebration of Splash Day had always been exciting for Leroy. It signaled the opening of the beaches for summer. The city hosted parades during the day, and there were fireworks at night. In the evening, there would be drinking, dancing and gambling. During the day, the women walked the beaches and competed in bathing beauty contests while the men competed in salt-water sea racing.

On that particular Splash Day, thousands of spectators in dark sunglasses with heads covered in sunhats, ball caps and holding umbrellas lined Seawall Boulevard facing the Gulf. Black binoculars protruded from under the shades of hats. Red, yellow, blue, and green sails on sailboats and the silver metal of yachts shone in the summer sun as boats paraded out in the Gulf, providing a colorful backdrop for the salt water sea race that was about to occur. Near Murdock's Bathhouse, a pleasure pier built on stilts over the Gulf, sailors stood with binoculars to watch the young athletes compete.

Leroy made the sign of the cross as he prepped for the race. He had a secret fantasy that his father, Peter, would pull strings for him in heaven and get God to give him some lucky breaks. He had been training for the race for weeks, but his stomach was tied in knots. He knew that ahead were rough waves full of stinging jellyfish and wind churning up the surf. It would be a rough swim, and it would take nothing short of a miracle to win this race.

Gazing out at sea, he saw a pod of porpoises, twenty or thirty of them, the sunlight gleaming off of their backs as they scissored in and out of the water. Leroy regained his focus on the race and looked at the man with the starting gun. He saw the referee's hand motion downward after the blast of the gun he could not hear.

Leroy shot forward. Thirty thousand pairs of eyes were on the anxious athlete.

The race was hard. The waves splashed in his eyes. He swung his arms like the sharp blades of a plow cutting into soft soil. Schools of jellyfish stung him on the legs and arms, but he pushed forward and passed even the stronger swimmers in the race. He made it to the finish line in record time. He climbed out of the water on the pier, faced the adoring crowds and pounded his chest like Tarzan.

This "Tarzan chest pounding" became his signature winning gesture, a ritual that caused *The Galveston News* to dub him "Tarzan of the Sea," a title he confirmed again and again by winning races and pounding his chest. He could not hear the thunder of their clapping, but he could see the jubilation on the spectator's faces. Leroy loved pleasing crowds of people, and on that particular Splash Day he had done just that.

In the afternoon men crowded back onto the beach to compete in horseshoes. A newspaper reporter from *The Galveston Daily News* wrote that from the sky, men in airplanes released colorful corks with numbers on them, so red, blue, green and purple corks bobbed in the sea-green water. Excited swimmers paddled into the surf to retrieve the corks, for each was numbered and corresponded to a door prize given out at Murdock's Bath House.

In the late afternoon, a ceremony was held on the beach. Leroy's name was announced as winner of the race. Leroy smiled and proudly walked up to get his silver trophy. He posed with a young woman in a bathing suit for the newspaper photo. Beaming with pride, his mother cut out the picture the next day and placed it in the Colombo family photo album.

During these Splash Day races, *The Galveston Daily News* reported that Leroy won the five-mile race five times. During the 20 years from 1927 to 1947, he accumulated more than 35 victories in swim races, most of them in the Gulf.

In one long-distance race in 1923, Leroy finished 19 minutes ahead of the swimmer nearest him. *The Galveston Daily News* reported that thousands in the crowd cheered the deaf lifeguard on as Leroy swam to a red buoy near the 21st Street Pier.

A year later, Leroy won another race where he beat Herbert Brenan, the Amateur Athletic Union National Endurance titleholder. A reporter noted, "Mr. Brenan could swim longer than anyone else without stopping. But Leroy beat him."

And on Labor Day in 1925, Leroy found himself again competing with Brenan, this time in the first annual 10-mile race, designed to be the crowning event of the season. For Leroy, it was another opportunity to excel. Fourteen people started the race from the groins at 7 a.m. that morning.

The swimmers passed the fishing pier at 21st Street, and Leroy took the lead. Three men in rowboats tried to stay with the swimmers. They had to give up staying with Leroy because he pulled ahead so fast. Leroy reached the jetties and started back half an hour ahead of Brenan, his strongest competitor. Leroy swam fast until he reached the groin and made a straight line for the beach outside of the breakers. The other swimmers, including Brenan, trailed him. Leroy crossed the line in 45 minutes, or nearly a mile ahead of Brenan, after making the race in 6 hours and 55 minutes. Leroy got up on the raft and smiled to the crowd. He looked fresh as a daisy even though he just finished a grueling race.

Gordon Allen, a Deaf reporter for *The Silent Worker*, noted that one of the judges, George (Dutch) Murdoch said, "Give that boy an experienced instructor, and he will make an enviable record in the swimming world." Murdoch continued his accolades for Leroy: "In this race, Leroy won the beautiful Texcomo Coffee Trophy. His picture appeared in the sports pages of all the leading Texas papers. His picture was carried on the sports page of *The New York Times* on Sunday following the event."

Leroy's swimming accomplishments garnered much attention. Reporters for *The Galveston Daily News* followed him and reported how he won races in pools and lakes across Texas and much of the United States. His race times were so competitive that the Chamber of Commerce talked of sending Colombo to England to train for the

Olympics, but the city could never get enough money together for travel funds. Community leaders hosted dances and dramatic performances to raise money for helping Leroy train for the Olympics. The city also asked for donations from large steamship companies, but not much ever came of these fund-raising efforts.

Leroy's swimming and racing skills were tested again in 1926 when he had a race in St. Louis, Missouri, in the Mississippi River. It was a ten-mile race, and swimmers from across the South were invited to compete in this event. Leroy began the race in the muddy water and swam ahead of the other swimmers. But then Johnny Weiss-muller, of Tarzan fame, pulled ahead of him. With determination, stamina and speed, Leroy pulled ahead, but in his fervor, he experienced a sharp pain in his shoulder. It wasn't until after the race that he found out he had dis-located his shoulder. But Leroy did not give up the race. Despite the sharp pains in his shoulder, he kept plowing through the muddy water until he reached the finish line. While he only came in eighth place, he still beat Johnny Weissmuller who had quit the race earlier, according to *The Galveston Daily News*.

During his Mississippi River race, Leroy was required to walk part of the way. However, he had severe cramps and Leroy said to a newspaper reporter, "When they told me to walk, I told my manager, Earl Galceran, that I couldn't stand to swim and walk too. The doctor told me it made my side hurt and gave me the cramps. I had walked about three-quarters of a mile when I got a cramp. I had to do my best for Galveston people. I did my best. I never want to give up that race. I didn't know anything about it. I fainted and they pulled me out of the water."

Troy Hill, a Deaf reporter from *The Silent Worker*, a popular Deaf periodical, called Leroy, "the Deaf King of the Gulf" whose ten-mile swimming record allowed him to win many races. "Colombo did well by winning the eighth place, for he suffered a sprained shoulder in Gym training before the race and also not being used to river water swimming he was a bit handicapped."

The Deaf community was proud of their athlete, and reporters from other Deaf periodicals frequently followed Leroy's races and wrote articles about him, sharing his victories with other Deaf people.

Leroy would continue to win the 5 and 10 mile races that were often held in Galveston. Since there was no TV, beach-goers needed sports entertainment, and it was up to the lifeguards to provide it. Since they were such excellent swimmers who trained every day, these lifeguards became the city's athletes. And for a decade, hundreds of spectators flocked to the beach, crowding on the piers and seawall to watch Leroy and the other lifeguards swim in competitions for money and trophies.

During one of Leroy's races, an elegant lady dressed in red with a red sunhat and large red satin purse sat on the pier, watching the race. When she saw Leroy win the race, she jumped up to clap her hands. She dropped her red purse, which plunged into the muddy water and sank to the sandy bottom.

Leroy saw the accident and swam to the pier to dive for the purse, but currents had carried it farther down the beach. After repeated dives, he retrieved the soggy satin purse and swam back to give it to the lady. She kissed him, and Leroy blushed crimson. Then Leroy jumped back into the water to swim beside his brother Cinto to give him encouragement. Cinto finished in fifth place. Leroy won the race and the $1,000 first prize. He took the family out to dinner that night.

Seawater racing was not just for young men swimming in calm waters. *The Galveston Daily News* reported that at age 42 Leroy competed in the choppy waters of the Gulf. Thousands of spectators lined the seawall to watch the race. Leroy's competition was Roy P. Sutter, a lifeguard from Dallas, a man Leroy had defeated five years before. Some of the viewers used powerful field glasses to watch the two famous swimmers.

When the two men dove into the rough and cold water huge swells came in at 30 miles per hour. Leroy and Roy swam neck and neck through the whole race with the crowd on the edge of their seats in anticipation. Just short of the finish line, Leroy sprinted ahead and maintained a five-yard lead to the finish line. The victorious Leroy climbed up the ladder of the pier and stood to face the crowds. In his standard pose, he beat his chest like Tarzan, and the crowds roared with approval. Then Leroy stopped. He leaned over to the ladder and helped Sutter up, warning him to watch out for the barnacles on the iron rungs of the ladder. The reporters the next day commented on Leroy's sportsmanship.

The swimmers were honored with a dinner at a restaurant that night, an event that included speeches of praise, a trophy, and a cash prize. On the way to dinner, Leroy asked the driver to stop so he could buy a bottle of Southern Select, his favorite brand of whiskey. Leroy told his fans and supporters at dinner that night that he beat Sutter because he had "trained on Southern Select" according to a reporter in *The Galveston Daily News*. The crowd loved it. Leroy wasn't only an athlete. His personality helped him ride the high tides of Galveston society, where he was respected, praised, and adored.

Leroy loved to entertain the crowds, and they, particularly the Deaf community, loved him in return.

As the years rolled on, Leroy maintained his reputation as a long-distance swimming champion who was known for his strength, stamina and endurance in the Gulf waters.

Sports records show that his place as a seawater racer is unparalleled in the sports history of Galveston. "It is doubtful if any deaf distance swimmer has ever approached Colombo's mark," wrote a Deaf writer in *The Deaf American* in 1974. "Unfortunately for the sports book, but extremely fortunate for the many people whose lives he saved, Colombo was never offered an athletic scholarship or went into serious training as is now in vogue. Instead he put his great talents to use as a lifeguard." And for this, he played an important role in the history of lifeguarding, according to an interview with Vic Maceo.

8

Leroy and the History of Lifeguarding

We are less afraid to be drowned than thou art.
The Tempest, William Shakespeare

Leroy's entry into life as a lifeguard on Galveston Island was preceded by a rich lifeguarding history dating back to China in the 18th century. Men and women who scanned the seas for drowning victims were historically called coast watchers, lifesavers, or surf men, noted Clayton Evans in his book, *Rescue At Sea: An International History of Lifesaving, Coastal Rescue Craft and Organizations.* Early lifeguards lived in buildings or rescue stations set up along the shoreline. Most were self-taught volunteers until lifeguarding became a paid profession.

Clayton Evans writes that the first recorded lifeguard group was started in the Yangtze River region of China in 1708. Set up as a humanitarian and volunteer group, the group was later supported by taxes. The name of the organization was "The Chinkiang Association for the Saving of Life." The Chinese developed boats specifically for rescues and created techniques to revive waterlogged victims brought to shore after boat accidents or during typhoons or floods.

Clayton Evans states that the Dutch and English followed the Chinese in the 1700s, establishing organizations to assist sailors and fishermen without life jackets or the ability to swim who toppled into the sea from their vessels.

Lifesaving came to the U.S. in 1789, when the Massachusetts Humane Society set up refuge houses along the coast for survivors of shipwrecks. In 1807, the Society set up the nation's first lifeguard station on Cape Cod, 1,901 miles from Leroy's Galveston beaches. Because drowning occurred regularly and became a public safety problem, the U.S. Congress in 1884 appropriated money to hire staff for lifeboat stations along the coastline, mainly to help shipwreck victims. In 1878 the U.S. Lifesaving Institute was established; it would later merge with the U.S. Cutter Service and become known as the U.S. Coast Guard.

According to Evans, by the 1890s on Cape Cod, New Jersey, and California beaches, open-water swimming became fashionable. In 1901, following the Hurricane of 1900, "George Murdoch began construction of a new bathhouse to be ready for the summer season." People had more leisure time and money and would head to the shore for bathing. Few people, though, knew how to swim. As more people in these resorts lost their lives in drowning accidents, cities began hiring "guards" for the beaches. And from these guards, heroes and heroines emerged in the drama of lifesaving.

Just as Galveston had Leroy Colombo, other beaches

had their own celebrated lifeguards. In early 1900, one of the most celebrated lifeguards was a woman—Ida Lewis (1815-1911). In *The Keeper of Lime Rock*, Lenore Skomal writes about young Ida, the daughter of the Lime Rock Lighthouse keeper in Newport, Rhode Island. Her father and mother were both disabled, so Ida took over the lighthouse duties. From 1859 to 1881, she rescued 18 people from near death. Their boats would capsize when they came into the harbor during storms and freezing weather, and Ida would cross the frozen sea to pluck the fishermen from the water. In other equally dramatic episodes, when she saw persons in distress holding on to their overturned boats, she left the lighthouse and jumped into her rowboat to rescue the victims.

The first "swimming tank" didn't open until April 1925, and prior to that, few people knew how to swim, writes Woody LaBounty in the *Ocean City Bulletin*. Swimming as a sport as Leroy knew it would not come into fashion until later. Ironically, even many sailors and fishermen men who spent their lives on the water could not swim.

When many of the resorts on the eastern shore saw the need to hire "guards," they hired policemen who would change into their swimming suits during the morning, then change back to their uniforms in the afternoon notes Skip Lee in *History of Lifeguarding*. It must have seemed a logical extension of policemen's duties to provide safety for citizens on in the water as well as on land. There were also beach volunteers like Leroy, people who worked for tips at concession stands, renting umbrellas and chairs, while monitoring the water for bathers in need of assistance.

Leroy's entry into lifeguarding came through a volunteer organization as well, The Surf Toboggan Club (STC). Around 1928, when Leroy was in his early 20s, he and Cinto and Nick were invited to join the other seasoned lifeguards on a Sunday afternoon for a three-hour long distance swim. If they could endure the waves and the stinging jellyfish to complete the swim, they would be rewarded by being inducted into the Surf Toboggan Club, and they could wear the coveted STC insignia. During this time, men wore two piece bathing suits consisting of bottom trunks and a sleeveless tee shirt. Members sewed the STC insignia letters on their tee shirts for all to see.

The Colombo boys had been practicing for the three-hour swim for years, training with the older lifeguards during Sunday exercises. They felt ready to prove themselves.

Leroy, Cinto and Nick jumped into the water and started to swim parallel to the shore. For three long hours, they swam. The older lifeguards followed the young swimmers in rowboats. During the third hour, the boys swam into a school of stinging jellyfish, and Cinto pleaded with his brothers to stop and get into the rowboat because he was fatigued and water-logged. They would not let him. Finally, all three completed the swim, with Leroy in the lead, and the three felt much pride in becoming part of the STC.

Established in 1926 by William Curry and Herbert Breneu, Jr., the STC was a prestigious club. It attracted the strongest swimmers on the beach. A reporter noted, "It was the only club of its kind in the city, and perhaps the only club of its kind along the entire Gulf coast."

The club encouraged not only swimming but physical fitness as well. The STC badge meant that a young man was held to the highest standards of sportsmanship and public service. Members even cleaned up litter on the beach and babysat children.

Leroy's membership in the STC was a highlight in his young adult life. He and the club members gave swimming lessons, and they maintained a first aid station. The STC organized competitive swimming races in the Gulf that attracted hundreds of locals and tourists. One reporter noted, "Among the swimming champions numbered in the STC membership is Leroy Colombo, the Gulf Coast ten-mile champion, and holder of the unofficial world record for 10 mile swim in six hours and 45 minutes."

The STC gave Leroy a community of men to share friendship and a profession, and even among these men, Leroy stood out.

Many commented on Leroy's uncanny ability to see swimmers in distress even as older guards shook their heads, not seeing, as Leroy did, heads bobbing far out in the water against the horizon line. Was Leroy's a supernatural gift, or was he less distracted from the noise on the beach because he was deaf? Was he an over-compensator? An overachiever? These questions were posed by psychologist Dr. Jim Marquette during an interview.

Today's science of lifeguarding provides clues. Leroy was an expert at eye scanning. Scientists of lifeguarding such as John Huntsucker in his *Engineering of the Eye and How It Impacts Lifeguard Scanning*, writes about the importance of the lifeguard's vigilance. He further explains that the lifeguard's head must be in constant motion with downward head swings in a systematic fashion to spot swimmers moving. John Huntsucker further notes that factors such as stress, fatigue, drugs and alcohol, and boredom can interfere with the lifeguard's scanning ability. Leroy had honed such skills in the years he spent observing other lifeguards on the beach. He had apprenticed himself to the best and became a competent lifeguard in his own right.

For Leroy, though, lifeguarding was more than a job. His fame came not only from the sheer numbers of people he saved from drowning but also from the manner in which he responded to distressed swimmers. Saving lives was his duty, which is partially why he scolded swimmers who swam out too deep. They didn't understand the power of the Gulf or the consequences of their own ignorance. But more than that, Leroy was selfless and egalitarian in his vigilance, once telling Dr. Jim Marquette in an interview:

> I not worry about my life. I go in lot dangerous and saved two fireman on top of E.S. Building used be hardware store. I do not give a damn about my life. I almost drown 16 times. God is always with me the time—I save Negro and Mexican or White people. I am not letting no damn people let color people drown. I save dog life got $25. Reward at Balinese Room. Will still save anybody life anytime. I do not make any difference. Dr. D. tell me to stay out of water & I am still expert swimmer.

Leroy made it evident that lifeguarding involved a physical engagement and gave him a sense of purpose beyond his own life. Saving lives made him feel alive. The Gulf was his natural element, and lifeguarding was his way of maintaining his proximity to it.

Except for the last seven years of his lifeguarding career from 1966 to 1973, Leroy served as a volunteer, earning nothing but receiving occasional tips and reward money for his daily efforts, according to Christie Mitchell writing in *The Galveston Daily News*. In 1966, when Leroy was put on the city payroll, he earned $1.00 per hour.

Lifeguarding wasn't exactly lucrative, and Leroy survived by finding odd jobs that kept him on or near the beach.

9

Living and Working on the Beach

I must go down to the sea again, to the vagrant gypsy life,
To the gull's way and the whale's way, where the
   wind's like a whetted knife.
                    "Sea Fever," John Masefield

Leroy's favorite work was at the beach, but he also worked other odd jobs as a dishwasher, a short order cook, an amateur boxer, a beach concession stand operator, a bouncer at the Balinese Room, and a night watchman for various nightclubs on Galveston Island, reported Leroy's nephew, Russ Colombo in an interview.

Because Leroy left the Texas School for the Deaf at 16, he did not complete high school and did not receive any professional or technical training. Teaching deaf children was a popular profession for the brightest deaf students, but such a career would have required Leroy to graduate from Gallaudet College. Another popular trade was print- ing. It attracted deaf people because they could withstand the loud noise of the early printing presses. Nick, Leroy's brother, was a printer, and it is likely that Nick may have invited his brother to join him. But Leroy loved the outdoors and didn't want to be confined to an indoor job if he could help it.

As a young boy, Leroy worked as a dishwasher for his Uncle Cinto at Gaido's Café, which was then located on Murdock's Pier. The pier had stores and restaurants lining it, and Leroy enjoyed being around the customers and being near the beach.

From the 1920s to the 1950s, Leroy worked with Nick's wife at a beach concession stand, renting chairs and umbrellas. They also sold hot dogs, hamburgers, and drinks—and all while Leroy watched the beaches, noted Russ Colombo in an interview.

For a number of years, Leroy lived on Stewart Beach in a large pavilion that had a small concrete structure designed to store beach umbrellas and chairs, writes Vic Maceo. The building had a bathhouse with a bathroom, a shower, and a room for changing clothes. Leroy kept a cot inside and called the small space his home for many years.

One newspaper reporter wrote that "Colombo once wrote about how he'd been able to live on the beach all of his life. While he couldn't hear the roar of the surf, he'd seen the sun and the water, and felt the sand between his toes every day."

As a young man, Leroy was also an amateur boxer. A reporter wrote, "Leroy Colombo, a Galveston mute, lost a one-fall match to Harry Johnson, a fellow citizen, in the opening prelim...the prelim boys were local boxers who had turned mat men for the occasion." But Leroy's mother did not approve of her son's boxing. When Leroy brought home prize money from his matches, she would take it and try to save it for Leroy. Expressing frustration with his mother, Leroy told Dr. Jim Marquette, "I used to try be prize fighter but my mother stopped me so I start swim and won all races in Galveston. I am still champion."

Leroy's favorite job, next to lifeguarding, was working as a bouncer at the Balinese Room. His physique made him an imposing figure. Here he could meet famous men and women entertainers. Leroy worked nights, escorting out rowdy customers who had too much to drink and who were loud and obnoxious, annoying the other guests. Sometimes he had to restrain them if the customers became feisty and pugnacious. He even punched a few in the nose after they started fights in the bar.

In the early 1920s, Galveston was vacation Mecca for the rich and the famous. The historian Gary Cartwright in his book, *Galveston: A History of the Island*, writes, "In its halcyon days, from the 1920s to the mid-1950s, the Boulevard was a glittering strip of casinos, nightclubs, and pleasure piers." As such, Galveston attracted lots of people who had money and leisure time, and this attracted young men like the Colombo boys, particularly Leroy.

The Balinese Room was a favorite among the movie stars, millionaires, and wealthy tourists who liked to gamble, drink, and listen to performers such as Frank Sinatra, Bob Hope, Peggy Lee, Gracie Allen, Jayne Mansfield, and Duke Ellington—all of which are pictured in a display at the Rosenberg Library on the Balinese Room.

Owned by Sam and Rosario Maceo, two men with Italian roots like Leroy, the Balinese Room was a thorn in city politicians' sides. The Maceo brothers had a network of informers at the police station and county courthouses, so it was nearly impossible for the city to close the illegal gambling house and prevent the sale and consumption of alcohol during Prohibition. In its heyday, the Balinese Room was decorated with fishnets, clamshells, and fabric-covered walls. It was strategically built on the end of a two-hundred-foot-long pier over the Gulf. The length of the pier allowed watchmen to see who was approaching, so the owners of the Balinese Room were able to warn their customers of raids from the Texas Rangers and the local police.

But the Rangers tried. One night, they assembled down the street, and one of the waiters informed the Maceo brothers. Since gambling was illegal, the Texas Rangers often came to the club to try catching gamblers in action. But when they arrived at the door, the waiter pushed a warning button, which alerted the bandleader with a flashing light, and he instructed his band to strike up the popular song, "The Eyes of Texas Are Upon You." This was the warning, and in seconds the gambling tables and slot machines folded into secret closets. The green felt-covered crap tables were covered with tablecloths and became bridge tables. Then came the announcement: "Ladies and Gentlemen, we give you in person, the Texas Rangers!"

Thwarted, the Texas Rangers increased their efforts, raiding the Balinese Room for 64 consecutive nights without a single bust. The infamous club was finally destroyed in a fire in 1953, and after reconstruction, its gaming rooms were closed in 1956. Hurricane Carla demolished it in 1961.

Too often Leroy's work was unpaid. Just as older, more experienced lifeguards mentored Leroy when he was young, so too did he train a new generation to keep watch over the Gulf.

When A. R. (Babe) Schwartz, a Texas state legislator and environmental lobbyist, was a boy of 12, he would meet Leroy at six in the morning at the lifeguard stand. Leroy and Babe brewed coffee for the other lifeguards, then they set up rental beach chairs and umbrellas for the day. Because the lifeguards trained every day before the crowds came to the beach in later morning, Leroy and Babe could take long early morning swims. They liked to swim several miles along the Gulf to the fishing pier, where groups of fishermen sat with poles stretched out like magic wands over the sea. The fishermen sat chatting and waiting for their daily catch. Leroy laughed and cut up with the fishermen, telling them in his deaf voice that he was stealing their fish.

Such a daily regimen of swimming developed the young Schwartz into a strong swimmer. He passed his swimming enthusiasm and skills along to his own sons. Schwartz reported, "Leroy didn't teach me how to swim, but he sure helped me develop my swimming endurance skills with those early morning workshops."

Throughout the day, the beaches filled with tourists and locals. The lifeguards rented them beach umbrellas and chairs and collected about $1.00 a day in tips. Occasionally, a mother would ask a lifeguard to babysit her children, and the lifeguards made extra income for this duty.

During an interview, Babe mentioned that Leroy taught him sign language when he was 13 years old. Babe told how he worked under Leroy as a junior lifeguard. Years later, Babe met Leroy at a favorite coffee shop. Babe reported that "the rest of the folks at the coffee shop must have wondered what we were laughing about and signing as we reminisced and laughed and how mad we made those fishermen on the 14th Street Pier when we bothered the fish with our swimming laps."

During the 1930s, a young local boy named Dorian Paskowitz was enamored of Leroy. Dorian's dream was to be a famous lifeguard, just like Leroy. As a youth, Dorian saw Leroy as "brown as a Hawaiian, muscular as a Greek god wearing a black bathing suit with a top cutout in the arm, standing like an Adonis on the lifeguard platform." To young Dorian, Leroy was a mythical figure sitting beside his brother Cinto who had the same dark Italian good looks.

During an interview, Dorian remembered meeting Leroy and being introduced to the surfboard and surfing. Leroy was a pioneer surfer and among the first to ride surfboards on Galveston beaches in the 1930s. Some even attribute Leroy as the first to bring surfing to Galveston Island—or at least the first to make it a popular sport. During this era in Texas, only Galveston had surfing. The other coastal areas such as Padre Island and Corpus Christi did not. Surfing was also becoming popular as a lifestyle in Hawaii, California, and Australia. On Galveston Island from 1932 to 1933, there were only three surfers, and Leroy was one of them.

For Dorian, surfing was "part of the beginning of my life of heaven on earth...the real joy of living." The first time that Dorian surfed he said, "It was on a very strange surfboard under the tutelage of a deaf-mute lifeguard, Leroy." As a youth, Dorian observed Leroy use the canvas-mat surfboards to save swimmers as well as to charm the beach crowds.

One day, Dorian watched Leroy as he grabbed his white, canvas surfboard and threw it off the lifeguard platform and into the foamy Gulf. He leaped off of the platform and paddled into the surf. At the right moment, he got on the surfboard, knees down, and positioned himself so he was facing the shore. When the right wave rolled in, he paddled furiously then raised to a standing position, balancing his muscular body. In that moment he and the surfboard seemed to be one. As he approached the shore riding the surfboard like a king, he leapt off of the surfboard and made a somersault into the air, landing on his feet. The beach crowds watched, anticipating such gymnastic feats. As he landed on his feet in the water, the crowd cheered, and in Leroy-fashion, he pounded his chest like Tarzan.

As a young boy, Vic Maceo, who years later retired as head of Galveston's Beach Patrol, said this about Colombo:

I knew him when I was a boy about 10 years old. He inspired me to become a lifeguard. The first time I met him, I was with my father and Leroy was a night watchman for Maceo properties. I had heard lots of stories about 'Dummy' Colombo from Ducky Prendergast. Dummy was a term of endearment, not of disrespect. Leroy took us under his wing. He had learned about the currents from his daily swims.

My memories of him were he used to walk up and down the beach with a whistle. When he saw swimmers out far, he would whistle and motion them in and then ball them out using his deaf speech. 'Too damn deep,' he would cuss at them and then he would kick them off the beach.

Leroy was also inspirational in indirect ways. As a youth, Peter Davis, Chief of Galveston's Beach Patrol, visited Ducky Prendergast, another famous Galveston life-guard and influential figure in life guarding history who saved hundreds of swimmers in Galveston during this same era. Prendergast told Davis stories, many of which involved his friend and fellow life guarding legend, Leroy Colombo. He gave advice that usually involved simple truths that speak volumes. One of his most frequent was, "You got to respect the water, son."

It was not only young hearing men that Leroy mentored, but young deaf men as well. In later years, Leroy was able to convince the Beach Patrol to hire two deaf lifeguards, the Kleberg brothers, who also had been students at the Texas School for the Deaf. They lived in Galveston, and Leroy often went to their house because their parents were Deaf and the whole family knew sign language. It was important, especially in those years, for the Deaf community to look after one another, and Leroy did just that in helping the Kleberg boys find jobs as lifeguards on the beach.

While he worked odd jobs during the days and nights, lifeguarding was never far from Leroy's mind. It was his keen visual and motion detection abilities as well as his competence in saving victims that created the hero, Leroy Colombo.

"He swam like a porpoise. His eyesight was so sharp," said D.L. Lack, Galveston's Police Chief. "He saved more people than I ever heard of or know of. He was, in my opinion, one of the greatest lifeguards that ever lived."

10

Rescues

Full fathom five thy father lies,
Of his bones are coral made;
Those are pearls that were his eyes;
Nothing of him that doth fade.
The Tempest, William Shakespeare

It was March, 13, 1928. Leroy sat on the pier gazing at the tugboat traffic in the bay. Suddenly, he felt strange vibrations underneath him. He looked out into the water, and to his horror saw wood, metal and glass violently hurled into the air before it came crashing down into the water. Had a bomb exploded?

About 25 feet away, a small, sturdy tugboat had collided with a large, flat-bottomed barge full of oil, sending red hot flames into the air.

Thrown backwards by the explosion, Leroy slowly stood up. He glanced over his shoulder and saw a cloth fire hose tightly wound around its case. When he reached for the fire hose, it fell apart in his hands. Rotten and rat-bitten, the hose was useless. All around him, billowing clouds of black smoke filled his lungs, choking him and filling his face with painful cinders that blinded him.

A man stood on the nearby smoke-filled wharf and waved frantically at Leroy. He pointed to two men who were in the fiery, oil-slicked water. Debris was burning everywhere— planks of wood, rubber, rope, bits of metal, and barrels. It seemed obvious that the men could not swim. They bobbed in the water with only charred faces showing, burned-off eyebrows and singed hair as evidence of the explosion. They clung to a broken wooden plank while desperately treading water. Sighting the two men, Leroy jumped in the water fully clothed and dove under the burning surface to the men. He circled one arm around one man and the other arm around the second, prying them from the splintery plank and kicking back toward the pier. Then Leroy spotted a third man, Fred W. Barr, the chief engineer of the tugboat, who clung to another plank nearby. Leroy swam to the pier with the two men, then returned to bring Barr to safety. Other workers had seen the accident and came down to the wharf to help Leroy get the three exhausted and shocked sailors onto the wharf.

A patrol boat picked up six other men who were floating in the sooty waters. But by himself, Leroy had saved two of the sailors from becoming badly burned and drowning in the harbor.

The inhalation of the smoke caused Leroy to begin coughing uncontrollably. He had swallowed some of the noxious gas from the explosion of the gas pipe, and he lay there spitting up phlegm.

Leroy reported to a newsman, "I don't remember clearly what happened after I got them as I had swallowed gas from the gas pipe which exploded and I was out of my mind for about 30 minutes. I could not eat or drink for 24 hours and the gas tasted like poison."

Not all of the men survived the tugboat explosion. One man panicked and jumped to his death in the burning debris, noted *The Galveston Daily News*.

Grateful for Leroy's heroic actions, the city councilmen convened a commission, and the men Leroy saved gave testimony. The city of Galveston wanted to award Leroy the Carnegie Medal of Honor. But surprisingly, one of the sailors recanted his story. He said that Leroy did not save him. He said that the sailors were able to use the plank and paddle to get to the wharf without Leroy's help. During this testimony, no witnesses came forth to support Leroy's heroic deeds. Leroy had a hard time following the conversations during the testimonies. He wished he had an interpreter in the courtroom, but he had no family members or lifeguard friends who knew how to sign.

The commission decided not to give Leroy the Carnegie Medal of Honor.

The wife of one of the sailors wrote Leroy a letter, "We cannot express our appreciation for what you have done for us. You have given me a husband, who I understand was nearly gone. For this, I can never repay you. Words cannot express how I feel about this matter. All I can say is I thank you."

Saving people and not receiving much appreciation was common in Leroy's lifeguard history. Once Leroy responded dryly to a news reporter, "The only reward I ever received was when I saved a dog from drowning. The owner gave me $25.00." In another instance, he saved a newsboy from drowning and the bystanders took up a collection of $1.00 to give him.

Bob Craig of the Ocean City Beach Patrol reported, "For their service, guards can expect a range of responses, from intense gratitude to indifference—or—embarrassment."

Despite these incidences of disrespect for putting his life on the line, Leroy, like other lifeguards did not let such bad behavior faze him.

During these early rescue years, Leroy was not the Lone Ranger on the beach, reported *The Galveston Daily News*. Leroy's colleagues were equally proficient in life-saving skills and they also saved hundreds of swimmers. A news reporter noted about one photograph of the patrol, "The eight tanned beach boys in the above picture are shown near Bill Curry's coaster station. These boys have saved hundreds of lives during the past several years. They help make the beach safe for bathers. These are Red Decker, Bill Curry, Budd Ewing, Cinto Colombo, S.A. Levy, Max Leman, Leon Weber, Ducky Prendergast, Cornelius Curry and Leroy Colombo. And when the boys are not saving lives, they usually can be found pitching horseshoes, playing ball, or showing a pretty girl how to swim."

Despite the tugboat incident, Leroy remained fearless in saving people from burning boats. One day he saw a shrimp boat burning near San Luis Pass, a narrow strait of water at the southwestern part of Galveston that connects Galveston Bay with the open Gulf.

The shrimp boat crewmen had jumped from the burning boat. They managed to reach a nearby island. A plane flying nearby attempted to rescue the men but could not land on the island. Leroy and other lifeguards swam to the island and cleared a place for the plane to land so they could rescue the men.

Leroy's lifesaving did not always involve dramatic fires. One day, a frantic mother ran up to the beach to Leroy. She cried that her children were lost and she could not find them. She told Leroy that she turned around to look for her sunglasses in her beach bag. When she looked up, the two young children had disappeared. Leroy touched her arm to reassure her. He explained that it was the long shore currents that pushed the children down the beach. Leroy took off down the beach. In an interview Sidney Steffans notes that lifeguards frequently found "lost" children at the beach and knew intuitively where to find them.

As he expected, Leroy found the two children in shallow pools of water about 200 yards down the beach where the currents had pushed them.

Rescues also happened in shallow water, noted Vic Maceo. Once Leroy saw a woman fully clothed walk into the surf. She stumbled and fell down into water over her head. Leroy jumped into the water and scooped her into his arms. He pulled her to shore and placed her face down in the sand, gently turning her face to the side. He pounded on her back to get her breathing again. Her husband, who was standing by his umbrella, came running to his wife. Another lifeguard called an ambulance, and Leroy climbed into the back and rode with her to the hospital. At the hospital she was treated for bruises and released.

It was the treacherous Gulf waters that forced Leroy to demonstrate his skill and bravery. Numerous times he pulled swimmers out of the deadly rip currents that move away from the beach, causing the water to become trapped between open waters and a sandbar or groin. Rip currents do not pull people under water, but they pull people away from the beach. Caught up in the rip current, most swimmers paddle vigorously to make it to shore. They fight against the current, become exhausted, sink and drown—unless a lifeguard swims out and saves them. Some estimate that 80 percent of water rescues are a result of rip currents. Leroy was there to save many a swimmer caught up in these rip currents.

During the 1940s many servicemen came to Galveston to relax and vacation at its clubs, bars, and beaches. Additionally, the U.S. military pumped up the economy by building a large army airfield with three large runways for army aircraft. Looking for fun and adventure, many of these soldiers in need of leisure activity came without their families. Often soldiers were more daring than the average beach goer. Arrogant and full of hubris, few of these young men listened to such authority figures as lifeguards.

One day, a soldier repeatedly climbed up Murdock's Pier and dove off the cross supports between the pilings. Leroy tried to convince the soldier to stop and to come down. He even ordered him to come down, but the man ignored Leroy. Foolishly, the soldier dove and broke his neck. Leroy pulled him out and took him to the hospital, but the soldier died the next day.

Another soldier, while swimming near the municipal

pier, lost his orientation and panicked in the water. He swam to the pilings and clung to the ones under the municipal pier until Leroy helped him come to shore. He suffered lacerations and bruises on his chest and body as the surf rocked him against the pilings.

During the war years, Leroy continued to save more soldiers, many of whom could not swim. Some, after drinking too much, went to the water to sober up and cool off, never to return to land.

Leroy's saves weren't restricted to his on-duty times, either. One afternoon, Leroy sat eating a hamburger on the 21st Street Pier Café. A tourist, recognizing Leroy, told him about a nearby swimmer in trouble. Leroy dove from the pier, pulled the limp body to shore and administered artificial respiration on the beach. An ambulance took the semiconscious man to the hospital, and Leroy accompanied him. The man survived.

Leroy's lifesaving attempts even involved automobiles. A reporter noted that when a car plunged off the Seawall, ejecting its surprised driver into the Gulf, Leroy ran after him and grabbed the dazed motorist who was heading haltingly toward the shore.

During Leroy's time, the beach was different from today's beach, according to Russ Colombo. The sand was a powdery white and only part of the Seawall had been built. People drove cars on the beach, and there was ample room for baseball games. The wooden groins, now stone jetties, were major swimming hazards. There were only two sandbars at that time. There were also deep holes 20 to 30 yards from shore that people could slip into unexpectedly.

Once, Leroy spotted a teenager who was caught in the currents. The current began to sweep the struggling youth against the pier. The boy tried to hold onto the pier, but the pilings were covered with barnacles. He slipped under the water.

Leroy grabbed his buoy and headed for the youth in trouble. He paddled out to him and grabbed him, placing the young man's arms on the buoy, and brought the boy to shore. Another lifeguard gave the boy a lecture on Gulf currents along the beach. According to a newspaper reporter, the boy from Houston commented to the lifeguards that swimming in the Gulf was different from swimming in a pool at home.

Leroy even saved whole families. One day, he noted that a mother swam out to the wooden groin to meet her son. When the mother arrived, she realized the boy was in danger as the waves had suddenly picked up and the boy was caught in a rip current. Desperately, she reached out for her son, but he pulled on his mother and both plunged under water. Another daughter noticed the two in distress and swam out to help. Leroy spotted the three swimmers, grabbed his buoy, and brought the three swimmers, one by one, back to the beach. The next day's newspaper reported that Leroy treated the mother and son with artificial respiration, and the daughter was treated for cuts and bruises.

Rip currents were not the only dangers. As a lifeguard on the beach, Leroy found the changeable waters quite challenging. It was not an easy body of water to decipher. On some days, on its surface, the Gulf was calm with rolling, gentle waves, and sometimes it lay perfectly still. But underneath its tranquil surface there were hidden holes, steep crevices, shifting sandbars, and razor-sharp barnacle-covered jetties. Then there were the stormy days on the Gulf when the rain hammered down and wind smacked boats against the piers, forcing swimmers and sunbathers to run for shelter. No matter what the weather was on the Gulf beaches, Leroy's skill as a lifeguard shone.

He also supported the other lifeguards, ready to help if necessary. When he was a junior lifeguard, Russ Colombo assisted his Uncle Leroy on the beach. One day as Russ tried to save a man, the man panicked and pulled Russ under. Right behind Russ was his Uncle Leroy who pulled both the man and Russ to shore. It was a close call for Russ, and he never forgot it.

Russ's mother, Leroy's sister-in-law, said this about Leroy: "He brought many back that are walking around today. He would work on a person and bring them back to life after others would say, 'There's no use.'"

"Drowning is a terrible death," said Vic Maceo, lifeguard and former head of the Galveston Beach Patrol. He reported this about his own experience of almost drowning:

> I was working the beach by myself one day. The surf was big. I went in for a rescue of two people near the rock jetty. I pushed the two people to the rocks and a fisherman pulled them out of the water. Suddenly a wave got me and pushed me under. I felt like a car wreck going down in slow motion. I had this feeling that I would not make it back up to the top. But my feet suddenly hit the bottom on the granite boulder. With my last breath, I pushed up hard and grabbed the rock above the water. The fisherman pulled

me in. Since then, the fear and horror of drowning never left me. I remember thinking, if I don't make it, I won't make it. Drowning is a terrible death. You go unconscious in about two minute but the panic in this final two minutes is terrible. The cause of the drowning is that you struggle and in that struggle you use up all your oxygen.

Vic Maceo said that in his 40 years of lifeguarding experiences, he witnessed many different reactions to persons drowning. "Some come up from under water and struggle. Others are not completely submerged. Others go under the water and never come up. There is no set number of times swimmers in distress go under and come up. Sometimes, a lifeguard may look out and see only a hand. Then the lifeguard has one chance to go in and save a life."

When lifeguards approached swimmers in distress, the swimmers were often in a full-blown panic. They would try to climb on the rescuer, hit or pull the lifeguard under. In the old days, Leroy and other lifeguards tried to stabilize such swimmers by knocking them out. In later years, they were trained to stabilize them by talking to them or telling them to hold on to a buoy.

The various challenges of saving made each time out a gamble, even for the strongest, and Leroy, one of the strongest, was not always successful in saving drowning swimmers.

A group of soldiers from Fort Crockett formed a swimming party one afternoon and went for a swim near 56th Street. Two of the soldiers left the group and swam 300 yards toward the wooden groins. One soldier was caught in the rip currents. The other soldier, seeing his buddy buffeted against the groin, swam over to help him. But he was unable to save his friend and clung to the groin until Leroy rescued him. He was bruised and suffered from cuts from the barnacles and from shock. His friend's body was found two hours later.

Another tragedy happened at Offatt's Bayou. One day, two men left early in the morning to go fishing in the bayou, a stretch of bay on the east end of Galveston. The men did not return that evening, and a search started the next morning when concerned family members called the police.

Leroy assisted lifeguards in retrieving their bodies. Neither fisherman knew how to swim, reported a newsman for *The Galveston Daily News*.

Another time, Leroy was sitting on the pier when he was told that two men had disappeared in the surf. Leroy swam 200 feet and dove for a man he saw go under. He located the second man and pulled the two to safety. One man had difficulty breathing, and Leroy could not revive him. The other man lived.

Leroy once told a reporter, "I almost drowned 16 times, I am lucky, thank God."

Leroy's record of saving 907 lives is recorded in the 1976 *Guinness Book of World Records* written by Norris and Ross McWhirter. The passage reads, "Life saving. November 1974, the City of Galveston and the Noon Optimist Club unveiled a plaque to the deaf mute lifeguard, Leroy Colombo (1905-74), who saved 907 people from drowning in the waters around Galveston Island, from 1917 to his death."

From young boyhood to adulthood, Leroy was drawn to the push and pull of the Gulf. He had sharp visual attention, motion detection, and acute concentration skills and was not distracted by noise, music or sounds. From age 12 to his 60s he could be found on the beach on almost any given day scanning the horizon for swimmers in distress. He pushed against calm or violent waves and across shallow as well as deep treacherous holes in the Gulf's muddy and sandy bottom to pull men, women, and children out of the Gulf as well as out of neighboring bays and bayous. His knowledge of the Gulf waters was extensive. Having spent a lifetime swimming, working and sleeping on the beach, he knew about the Gulf's tides, her erratic current patterns, her deadly behavior around the wooden groins and rock jetties, and her changing weather.

When a reporter asked Leroy, then in his 60s, how much longer he would be a lifeguard, Leroy replied, "As long as I live."

The Mature
Leroy Colombo

Leroy on the left and brother
Cinto on the right

11

Leroy's Deaf Community

"Deaf People Can Do Anything, But Hear."
—I.K. Jordan, First Deaf President of
Gallaudet University, 1988

The sky was blue and filled with a patchwork quilt of heavy white clouds. Leroy had spent much of the morning alert to changing beach conditions. He knew exactly where the sand bars began and ended. He knew where the holes in the sand beds were, along the rocky groins. He paid special attention to these danger zones.

Leroy was chatting with a group of deaf friends who came in from Houston to enjoy the day at the beach and to see the famous lifeguard Leroy Colombo. In their homes were copies of Deaf periodicals such as *The Silent Worker* and *The Deaf American*, which had articles about Leroy's lifesaving abilities as well as about his seawater racing times, records that no one in the South had beaten.

Out of the corner of his eye, Leroy saw a group of six deaf men in knee-deep water near the rocky groins. He knew they were deaf because he had talked with them most of the morning, catching up on Deaf sports and other Deaf community news. Now they were cooling off in the surf with hundreds of other swimmers who were crowded together in the water, swaying back and forth with the movement of the waves.

The tide was coming in fast. Leroy glanced at the men and saw that two of them were struggling. A perpendicular current of fast-moving water had come in with the tides. The sides of the wooden groin provided a tunnel, and swimmers were caught in the rip currents that pulled them down into the Gulf water. He knew the deaf men would not hear his whistle, but he blew it anyway to alert the other lifeguards on the beach. He might need their help.

Leroy grabbed the metal, octagonal buoy and raced into the water. He reached two of the men and dragged them to safety. Then he went back for the other four men, two at a time, and brought them safely to shore.

Such stories quickly spread through the Deaf community. Leroy was their "favorite son," their hero. Even though Leroy was chided by his deaf friends for flirting with women, showing off his trophies and scrapbooks, he was cherished as a friend, according to Jerry Hassell. Deaf people flocked to Galveston beaches looking for the Deaf lifeguard, hoping to spend time chatting with him. People in the Deaf community respected not only his accomplishments but his ability to convince the Beach Patrol to employ as lifeguards two of his deaf friends, Marcus and Robert Kleberg. Leroy relished these visits from his Deaf friends.

The late Jerry Hassell, a beloved reading teacher from the Texas School for the Deaf and tireless advocate for the Deaf community in Austin, traveled by car with his mother and father from Houston to go to Galveston's

Beach when he was a youth and recalls those days:

> When I was a teenager about age 14 in 1942, my parents took me to Galveston in the summer to swim. I was surprised to find a lifeguard at Gal-veston who used sign language. When I learned that he was a deaf person, I was absolutely astounded. Even more than that, I was flab-bergasted when he told me that he attended the Texas School for the Deaf at one time. For the next 8 summers, I continued to see Leroy often while he was on duty and had the chance to talk to him many times. I knew that two of my friends, Robert Kleberg (TSD, class of 1942) and his brother Marcellus Kleberg (TSD, class of 1943) worked at the same beach renting out beach umbrellas and chairs. I even remembered that Malcolm Pace, my classmate was actually saved from drowning by Leroy.

Jerry Hassell reported that "Colombo had an eye for the ladies and he was always flirting. He liked to be the center of attention." From 1935 to 1945, Leroy drank a lot and was overweight in his old age. Colombo also bragged a lot and was not very well liked by the younger Deaf crowd. But he was admired by the older Deaf crowd because of his racing and lifesaving skills.

Marcellus Kleberg, a former deaf lifeguard at Galveston, remembers Colombo very well as they were not only friends but also coworkers:

> I've known him since I was a little boy. I was a lifeguard for two to three summers from 1944 to 1945. I became one of the first deaf lifeguards with Leroy under the Galveston Beach Patrol. Leroy was complaining once about his job. The captain warned him not to drink liquor while he worked. Finally, we both got a real job as a lifeguard and got paid. He saved a lot of people, more than 500.

Another deaf friend (TSD class of 1942) Early McVey was a youth when he lived in Houston. He remembers this about Colombo:

> I would drive to Galveston from Houston with a group of deaf friends for the day to have a picnic and to swim at the beach. We would often visit Leroy during the summer. We saw him patrolling the beach. We also saw him during swimming races in the Gulf. We would often stop and chat with him because he knew sign language."

Early McVey became president of the Fraternal Society of the Deaf (FRAT), which provided insurance to its members as other insurance companies denied deaf people coverage. Leroy lapsed in paying his FRAT dues, and when he developed a stomach ulcer in later years, he asked the FRAT for help with medical expenses. In an interview, McVey stated, "Leroy contacted me when he was ill and he asked for help with his lapsed insurance dues. So I got together with some FRAT members who contributed and paid his dues so he could get health insurance benefits."

Since the 1920s, hearing journalists have pumped up stories about Colombo with hyperbolic prose. His many monikers could compete with a Greek mythology text:

—the deaf and dumb eagle-eyed swimming marvel
—Tarzan of the Sea
—the deaf-mute ace swimmer
—the Champion Swimmer of the South
—strong, sinewy and burnt to a nut brown
—suntanned deaf-mute
—crack local distance swimmer
—deaf-mute guard of the Beach patrol
—aquatic star
—best-liked character on the beach.

But depicting him as a celebrity on the entertainment circuit or as a heroic action cartoon figure can mask the "low tides" that also characterized Colombo's life: poverty, loneliness, isolation, and health issues, including stomach ulcers and a bleeding esophagus brought on by alcohol and heart disease. One reporter noted, "Even in the 1960s, he was working for $1.00 an hour during the tourist season and was making ash trays out of seashells to get through the winter."

During Leroy's time there were no videophones that could connect him to his deaf friends in Houston or Austin. Sign language interpreter services were nonexistent during Leroy's time. Typically a family member learns sign language and becomes the deaf person's interpreter, but no one in the Colombo family learned sign language; neither did his lifeguard colleagues, except for Babe Schwartz.

Depicted as a superhuman figure persona by news reporters of his day, Leroy continues to be an enigma. Was he the romantic hero, the high-spirited quipster with the tan, muscular physique, the cigar-smoking, whiskey-toting, babe-holding rake? Or was he the trophy-collecting glamour boy as served up for readers in *The Galveston Daily News*?

Leroy's personal side was better known in the Deaf community, a community that is isolated by the very nature of the fact that few people know sign language. When Leroy arrived at the Texas School for the Deaf, he was immediately accepted into the clannish but protective community of persons with similar experiences living in a largely insensitive, hearing and speaking world. Warm, friendly photos from the Texas School for the Deaf and those printed in Deaf periodicals show Leroy with a smiling face alongside his deaf classmates. Other affectionate photos show him leisurely posing with groups of his deaf friends, linked arm-in-arm, along with reports of his attending sporting and social events hosted by the Houston chapter of the FRAT.

There are also pictures of Leroy palling around with his buddy Fred "Dummy" Mahan, a boxing champion who fought at Galveston and who was also a former student at the Texas School for the Deaf. Captions to photos and writing in the Deaf periodicals contain affectionate words such as "A Crowd of Deaf Folks on the Beach at Galveston." There are also descriptions of Leroy and Dummy Mahan as "Two Silent Lads Who Went Up the Ladder of Fame."

Referring to a meeting Colombo attended at The Houston Silent Club, the Deaf writer reports, "They are still coming to, one by one, and Houston's population of deafies is growing gradually, and the first thing you know Houston will be in the rank of all other cities that deserve recognition of being the place for prosperity for the coming generation of Deafdom."

Affectionate and sentimental words about Colombo came from the writings of deaf journalists. In another edition of *The Silent Worker*, a deaf writer reports that Colombo had "a brown and tanned face, big red sinewy hands, and the smoothness of his signs indicated he was a perfect athlete."

A caption under a picture of Colombo holding a large trophy reads, "Leroy Colombo and his half-acre smile of victory." And still another, "After the Victory, Leroy Colombo is being carried from the water by his brother clubmen." The periodical even printed a poem written by Leroy's sister that captures the affection people had for Leroy. The poem is partially excerpted here:

> But only one could win you know,
> And this honor went to the champ Colombo
> The crowd yelled praise to their aquatic brother,
> But none meant so much as the praise of his mother
> Who was patiently waiting for him to come in,
> For he told her on leaving, "I'm going to win."

In contrast to these warm, family-like albums of pictures and articles found in the Deaf periodicals, hearing newspaper journalists and his relatives emphasized his greatness as a racer and lifesaver but also discussed his "affliction of being deaf and dumb since seven." One mentioned him as "a man who strains a great deal to make his broken language understood," and several mentioned his "muttering speech."

Reporters repeatedly describe him as "the deaf-mute." Yet Leroy was not mute. He could talk, as he lost his hearing at age 6 after he had already learned to speak. But his speech had deteriorated because he could not hear it.

Such negative images as being a "deaf mute" or "afflicted" or having "broken language" were not found in the Deaf community's writings about Leroy. For Leroy's Deaf friends, he had no affliction, no broken language. Leroy's lack of speech and hearing simply did not matter. Among his Deaf friends, he did not need to talk. Sign language was more than sufficient; it was better. When he was with other Deaf friends, he fit in, and there was no struggle to communicate as there was with hearing people who could not sign.

His Deaf friends remember him fondly and affectionately as a friend and as the man they loved and admired for his athletic ability, life saving rescues and friendly personality.

Leroy could do anything on the beach, except hear.

12

Last Lap

And all I ask is a merry yarn from a laughing fellow-rover,
And a quiet sleep and a sweet dream when the long
    trick's over.
                              "Sea Fever," John Masefield

Russ Colombo once described his uncle as the type of man who "would give anyone the shirt off his back." Yet unlike most about whom this is said, Leroy fully embodied the selflessness the phrase describes. He had three passions: the Gulf, swimming, and helping others.

The Gulf had given him back the use of his legs after the temporary paralysis brought on by meningitis in his youth. Leroy returned the favor, daily risking his own life to save people from the waters that had done so much for him. He was a part of the Galveston community in ways that most were not, entrenched as a figurehead and well known by all.

Leroy's family was loving. Russ recalled that when he was young, he and his brothers often rode their bicycles over to the Colombo home on 21st Street. Leroy didn't live there, but three of Leroy's sisters did. Nettie, Catherine, and Esther would "welcome the boys and spoil them with cookies and candy, and they were cooking something good all the time." The sisters were proud of Leroy, and Leroy's brothers would cut up and swear while playing cards and drinking Southern Select and Pearl beer.

Leroy's social life didn't seem to suffer much, either, and Leroy hung out on the beach, in the bars and clubs, and in restaurants. He played horseshoes with millionaires and bums on the beach.

One of Leroy's friends, Dr. Jim Marquette, remembers meeting Leroy at D.J.'s Bait Shop in the early 1970s. The bait stand, on the west end of the island near the seawall, was started by Ina, a lady who retired and moved to Beaumont in her later years. She found keeping live bait to be too much work, but keeping beer was easy, so the bait shop was more of a dive and attracted a group of regulars who stopped to have a cold beer on hot summer days.

Marquette recalls his first encounter with Leroy:

A big flurry occurred at the entrance. A big hefty smiling bald-headed fellow entered, and there was a flurry of hand waving and backslapping. Who was that? That was Leroy Colombo. He came in and visited with everyone. He was a delightful and charming fellow. I never had a problem getting him to understand me. He read lips. He had some moderate ability of grunting speech. Reading my lips, and listening to his coarse speech, he could make himself known. I would frequently visit him over about two years, I think it was 1971 to 1973. I lived in Galveston at the time. Now, I have met people who impressed me because of their accomplishments. This man was one of them.

Leroy was a magnet, and people sought him out. To celebrate his fame, one tavern put up a sign, "Colombo's Records," and the wall boasted Leroy's record times for his races, ranging from one mile to thirty. They also posted information on his saves. 835 people. One dog.

These statistics were talking points whenever Leroy frequented the tavern.

But Leroy never had a permanent address according to his lifeguard friends Vic Maceo and Bill Scott. He slept on the beach on a cot in the concession stand or slept in his car parked on the Seawall. A fire once destroyed Leroy's personal belongings when he stayed at a friend's house.

There is no official record of marriage, though local rumors have it that Leroy married three times—once to a millionairess—and that all ended in divorce.

Though most who came into contact with him noted Leroy's ability to communicate well, language was still a barrier. Leroy was frequently frustrated that he could not communicate easily with his friends and family. The Texas School for the Deaf had given him a taste of Deaf culture, and he had gained a Deaf identity, finding himself in a community of people who were like him. He was able to learn American Sign Language, and he made friends that he would keep in contact with for a lifetime.

Jerry Hassell met Leroy when Jerry was a teenager. Jerry said that "Leroy was aloof to the Deaf community in later years. He stayed near the beach."

Many of Leroy's Deaf friends lived outside of Galveston, though, and he may not have been able to afford the gas to drive to Austin, Houston, or Dallas, where large numbers of Deaf people congregated for conventions.

In 1964, Harry Lang, author of *A Phone of Our Own: The Deaf Insurrection Against Ma Bell* wrote that the TTY or teletype telephone was invented by the Deaf engineer/

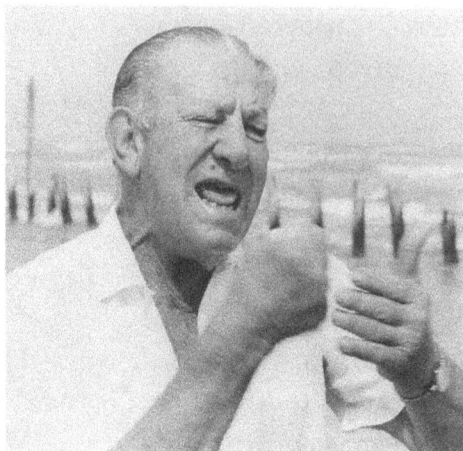

The elder Leroy Colombo struggling
to communicate

Deaf since age 6, Leroy Colombo mastered American Sign Language (ASL) as well as fingerspelling, though none of his family members did so, and only one of his hearing friends learned ASL. So in the world of the hearing, Colombo struggled with communication for most of his life.

LEROY PETER COLOMBO
DEC. 23, 1905 —— JULY 12, 1974
A DEAF-MUTE WHO RISKED HIS OWN LIFE
REPEATEDLY TO SAVE MORE THAN A THOUSAND
LIVES FROM DROWNING IN OUR ISLAND WATERS

Leroy Colombo was deaf, but he was not mute. But people found his speech odd because he could not monitor and correct his speech after he became deaf. His family said he spoke in his "deaf voice."

inventor Robert Weitbrecht. But in 1964, Leroy had no home in which to install a TTY. Without video technology, cell phone and email advances, Leroy had no easy way to contact Deaf friends.

The Deaf press frequently wrote about Leroy, even in his later years, and he is mentioned in *The Silent Worker, Digest of the Deaf, The Deaf American,* and *The Deaf American Monographs*. All chronicled his contribution to Deaf community sports. He was featured in Jack Gannon's *Deaf Heritage: A Narrative History of Deaf America,* Robert and John Panara's *Great Deaf Americans,* and Catherine Carroll and Sue Mather's *Twenty-Six Tales of Genius, Perseverance and Heroism: Movers and Shakers That Changed the World.*

Leroy Colombo's feats were legendary, even among his Beach Patrol cohorts, and he was mentored by the best and mentored the best. Henry de Vries, Charles Bertolino, Ducky Prendergast, Red Decker, Bill Curry, Budd Ewing, S.A. Levy, Max Leman, Leon Webe, Cornelius Curry, and Cinto Colombo all made records saving swimmers from drowning in the Gulf. Vic Maceo and Bill Scott were mentored by Leroy as well, and both are heroes themselves, having saved hundreds of people from drowning.

While Leroy spent some of his life away from Galveston beach, Ducky Prendergast pointed out that "Leroy's life was on the beach—and it was for his sixty-eight years."

Riddled with bad health, restless and reclusive, Leroy entered the twilight of his 40-year distinguished lifeguard career alone and without means. For four decades he was a powerhouse on the beach. He was depicted in the media as a hero, one for whom races, streets, markers, and monuments would be named in his honor. He had made his city proud, and *The Galveston Daily News* documented it all.

But Leroy lived in an era when a deaf person's intellectual potential was not recognized, and the deaf had no legal protections such as those guaranteed later by the Americans with Disabilities Act. Deaf people did not have sign language interpreters, captioned television, modifications at school, or technology such as videophones. Access to higher education was rare.

Only one of his friends A.R. (Babe) Schwartz learned sign language, and none of Leroy's surviving relatives and friends remember ever seeing Leroy use sign language with others.

During Leroy's era, few people learned sign language. Lipreading was emphasized, and there was a stigma to sign language. Therefore, much of Leroy's communication with those in his life was superficial at best, and he may have internalized, then suppressed, the negative impression of his own language.

Like many an aging athlete whose youthful popularity is based on physical attractiveness, athletic ability, and image, Leroy spiraled downward as he grew older.

In his youth, beer was the champagne of the young beach bathers, the lifeguards, movie stars, and tourists. Sidney Steffans, a former lifeguard who became a marine biologist said, "After a long day of guarding swimmers, beer released tension." It also provided extra energy for that last lap. And beer and whiskey filled the lonely evening hours at taverns and improved Leroy's storytelling abilities as he recounted his races.

Today, alcoholism is considered a disease that warrants medical and psychological treatment. But while Alcoholics Anonymous (AA) support groups emerged in the 1930s, these meetings were not accessible to the Deaf. There were no sign language interpreters, and even if there had been, Leroy would not likely have known of such support or sought help.

After a lifetime of social drinking, at 68 years old Leroy was in poor health. He visited a friend one night and complained of chest pain. According to Russ Colombo, the friend called an ambulance. Grizzled, unshaven, and bloated, Leroy had been living in a back room behind a bar in Galveston where a friend allowed him to sleep.

A doctor from St. Mary's Hospital called the home of Leroy's brother, Nick Colombo. Leroy's sister-in-law came to the hospital because Nick was recuperating from a stroke and was bedridden.

When she arrived at the hospital, the doctor told her that Leroy was dying of heart complications and severe esophageal bleeding brought on by years of excessive drinking.

On his deathbed, Leroy told friend and fellow lifeguard Bill Scott to take his station wagon for the Beach Patrol. Bill followed orders, and Leroy's station wagon continued to help the Beach Patrol in its duties until the last cylinder gave out.

Leroy's death certificate lists the cause of death as arteriosclerotic cardiovascular disease. His date of death:

Friday, July 12, 1974.

At the time of Leroy's funeral, his nephew Russ Colombo was a young man, a student at the University of Houston. He immediately came home to help his mother plan his Uncle Leroy's funeral. Russ was one of the pall-bearers.

The night before the funeral, family and friends met at the funeral home to say the rosary. The next day, funeral services for Leroy were held at St. Mary's Catholic Church, where he and his brothers and sisters were baptized. He was survived by his brother Nick and his sister Catherine.

Legendary in life and death, Leroy's name was widely known, and a Deaf writer for *The Deaf American* wrote, "The thousands of young swimmers who crowd Galveston Island's pleasure beaches hardly noticed his passing; but old-timers on the Gulf, veteran sports writers, and the Deaf community paid tribute to an authentic hero."

In an interview, Russ Colombo reported that after the funeral Mass, forty cars formed a procession with a police escort and a fire truck to Calvary Cemetery. Then the long black hearse that contained Leroy's casket stopped and took a turn to the left and headed for the beach. Instead of following the road to Broadway Avenue and the cemetery, the procession ended up on the beach sands. The people in the cars were puzzled by the change in direction. When the hearse got to the beach, it stopped briefly for a moment of silence so that Leroy could have one last moment on the beach.

IN MEMORY OF
LEROY COLOMBO
DECEMBER 23, 1905 - JULY 12, 1974
"A DEAF-MUTE" WHO RISKED HIS OWN LIFE REPEATEDLY
TO SAVE MORE THAN A THOUSAND LIVES FROM DROWNING
IN THE WATERS SURROUNDING GALVESTON ISLAND
PLAQUE DEDICATED
NOVEMBER 1974
BY THE
NOON OPTIMIST CLUB
AND THE
CITY OF GALVESTON, TEXAS

Outside of Leroy Colombo's Deaf community, few had much understanding of the difficulty Leroy Colombo faced in communicating with a hearing world. People referred to him as a "deaf-mute," a term abhorred by the Deaf community. The fact that Colombo was not mute did not stop many from applying the term to him, even in this memorial erected by people who knew him.

56	The Texas Deaf and Dumb Asylum was established by the Texas legislature in Austin, Texas.
80	The National Association for the Deaf (NAD), the Deaf community's Civil Rights organization created by and for Deaf people was established.
01	Theordore Roosevelt begins U.S. presidency (1901-1909)
05 c. 23	Peter Leroy Colombo born to Italian-American immigrants, Peter Colombo (1863-1913) and Catherine Gaido Colombo (1873-1944) at St. Mary Hospital in Galveston, TX. Colombo's mother was born in Torino, Italy and his father was born in Milan, Italy.
09	William Howard Taft becomes U.S. president (1909-1913)
10	Edward Miner Gallaudet retires as president of Gallaudet University (then The Columbia Institution). Gallaudet University is a liberal arts university for the deaf in Washington, D.C. Its archive library houses articles about Colombo.
11	Gaido's Café opens on Murdock's Bathhouse. Cinto Gaido is the brother of Leroy's mother, Catherine.
12	Epidemic of meningitis spreads through Texas and Leroy contracts it becoming deaf and partially paralyzed
	Leroy attends Sam Houston Elementary School in Galveston
	Galveston ships out 4 million bales of cotton and is one of the largest ports in U.S.
13	Woodrow Wilson begins U.S. Presidency (1913-1921)
	Leroy's father dies of a heart attack at age 54 leaving behind a wife and 8 young children.
14	Leroy continues his studies at Sam Houston Elementary School, Galveston. World War I begins (1914-1918)
15 ug 23	Leroy's mother enrolls him into the Texas School for the Deaf in Austin, called then the Texas Deaf and Dumb Asylum.
16	A new library and auditorium are built at the school.
17	**Edward Miner Gallaudet, former president of Gallaudet College dies in Hartford, CN**
18	At age 12 and ½, while home from TSD during the summer, Leroy saved his first life on Galveston beaches.
19	Hurricane hits Galveston Island
20	**Population: Galveston County 53,150; Galveston City 44,255.** **While in Austin at TSD, Leroy frequently swam with his deaf friends at Bull Creek and Barton Springs Creek.** During 1920's Magnolia Willis Sealy planted oleanders all over the Island and this became Galveston's official flower.

1921	Warren G. Harding begins U.S. Presidency (1921-1923) Leroy joined brothers, Cir and Nick as volunteer lifeguards in Surf Tobaggan Club. Leroy was the strongest swimmer, swam 15 miles in 11 hours
1922	**Leroy left the Texas School for the deaf. Went back to home in Galveston.** **Alexander Graham Bell, the inventor of the telephone and proponent of the speech only method to teaching of the deaf dies.**
1923	**Calvin Coolidge becomes U.S. President (1923-1929)** **Colombo became a full-fledged volunteer lifeguard for the city of Galveston.** **From 1923 to 1926, Colombo took part in a number of distance races from 10 30 miles in length. In two races, he defeated the American Athletic Union's (AAU) national endurance champion, setting new records as he was winning**
1924	**Leroy won his first race when he beat Herbert Brenan, the Amateur Athletic Union. National Endurance Champion in a one-mile race.**
1925	Leroy won his first long distance swimming race, 10-mile and set a new record in Galveston by finishing the race in 6 hours and 55 minutes. Colombo won coveted Texcomo Coffee Trophy. **Leroy and Cinto, his brother were elected to STC and became member of Firs Aid LifeGuard Squad.**
1926	Leroy swam in race in St. Louis, Missouri in Mississippi River. Dislocated his shoulder but stayed to complete the race. Johnny Weismiller of Tarzan fame, also swam in this race but quit before finishing.
1928	On Pier 20, Leroy saved two men, the Captain and First-Mate from a tug boat Propeller which exploded and caught fire when it sank after a collision. Colombo dived in the icy waters of March and rescued them before the authorities arrived.
1929	Herbert Hoover began his U.S. Presidency (1929-1933)
1930	Man was seized with cramps in Crystal Palace Pool. Leroy saved him from drownin Population: Galveston County 64,401; Galveston City 52,938.
1933	Franklin Delano Roosevelt becomes U.S. President (1933-1945)
1935	One of Leroy's proudest possessions is a letter from a Dallas woman, whose brother was saved in Galveston
1937	Leroy won $500 in 5 mile race. Then he dived into water to retrieve a woman's lost purse in the water. President Franklin D. Roosevelt visits Galveston.

39	Leroy and Marcus Kleberg, another Deaf lifeguard were members of the Beach Patrol. World War II begins (1939-1945)
40	Population: Galveston County 81,173; Galveston City 60,862.
42	Leroy saves many U.S. soldiers lives from drowning.
44	Catherine Gaido Colombo, Leroy's mother dies.
45	Harry S. Truman begins his U.S. Presidency (1945-1953) Leroy saved four swimmers near the municipal pier. (April 22, 1945) Leroy was not able to save one woman who drowned. He had a record of 38 failed attempts of saving drowning swimmers. (April 29, 1945)
47	Texas City Disaster: explosion and fire kill 512 people. Army closes Fort Crockett after 50 years in Galveston
49	Hurricane hits Galveston Island
50	Korean War begins (1950-1953).
53	Dwight D. Eisennhower begins his U.S. Presidency (1953-1961)
54	The Columbia Institution is renamed Galladuet College by Act of Congress. U.S. Supreme Court outlaws segregation forcing colored schools for the deaf to close and integrate with institutions serving white children.
957	**Texas Rangers close down Galveston's illegal gambling casinos.** **Hurricane hits Galveston Island**
958	President Dwight D. Eisenhower signs P.L. 85-905 establishing Captioned Films for the Deaf.
960	Population: Galveston County 140,364; Galveston City 67,175.
961	President John F. Kennedy begins his U.S. Presidency (1961-1963) Hurricane Carla hits Galveston County.
963	JKF assassinated. Lyndon B. Johnson begins U.S. Presidency (1963-1969)
964	Robert H. Weitbrecht invents a terminal unit which permits Deaf people to use teletypewriters to send messages over the telephone.
965	The Texas Blind, Deaf and Orphan School for the Colored was integrated into the Texas School for the Deaf
967	Leroy retires from lifeguard job.
969	Richard C. Nixon begins his U.S. Presidency (1969-1974) Viet Nam War begins (1969-1975).
1970	Population: Galveston County 169,812; Galveston City 61,809.
1973	Section 504 of the 1973 Rehabilitation was passed. This Act bans discrimination on the basis of disability by recipients of federal funds.

1974 July 12	Leroy dies of a heart attack. Services were conducted for Leroy at St. Mary's Catholic Church. He was buried in Calvary Cemetery, Galveston.
	Shortly after Colombo's death, the Texas Senate in Austin stood for a moment of silence in his honor. July 18, City of Galveston passed a resolution honoring Leroy Colombo. **National Association of the Deaf (NAD) does census of deaf Americans; counts 13.4 million hearing impaired and 1.8 million deaf Americans.** The Noon Optimist Club and the City of Galveston erected a monument erected on 51st and Seawall Blvd. to honor Leroy Colombo. Gerald Ford begins his U.S. Presidency (1974-1977).
1975 Apr. 25	**Texas Senate sponsored a Senate Resolution (S.R No. 49) in the memory of Leroy Colombo by A.R. (Babe) Schwartz and also ordered the lowering of the state flag.** P.L. 94-142 Education for All Handicapped Children was passed. This would later become the IDEA (Individuals With Disabilities Act), amended in 1990, 1997, 2004.
1976	Leroy Colombo cited in *Guinness Book of World Records*.
1977	Jimmy Carter begins his U.S. Presidency (1977-1981)
1978	Dr. Gertie Galloway becomes the first Deaf woman President of the National Association for the Deaf.
1981	Ronald Reagan begins his U.S. Presidency (1981-1989) The Texas School for the Deaf became an independent school district and was made a state resource center for other deaf education programs in the state. Dr. Victor Galloway became the school's first Deaf superintendent.
1986	Gallaudet College becomes Gallaudet University when President Ronald Reagan signs the Education of the Deaf Act (Public Law 99-371).
1988	Deaf President Now Movement (DPN), a Deaf Civil Rights movement, brings about change with the selection of I.K. Jordan, the first Deaf President of Gallaudet University in its history.
1989	George Bush begins his U.S. Presidency (1989-1993)
1990	The American With Disabilities Act (ADA) was signed by President George Bush. This is the Civil Rights Act for Deaf and disabled U.S. citizens.
1993	Bill Clinton begins his U.S. Presidency (1993-2001)
2001	George W. Bush begins his U.S. Presidency (2001-2009)
2002	Leroy was inducted in Texas School for the Deaf Athletic Association (TSDAA) Sports Hall of Fame at the Texas School for the Deaf
2004	Exhibition featuring Leroy, the surfer, is shown at Texas Surf Museum, Corpus Christi, Texas.
2006	Texas School for the Deaf names new natatorium after Leroy Colombo during their 150th year celebration.
2008 May 20	Galveston City Council renames a two-block stretch of 57th Street as View and 57th Street. The city also erects a historical marker about Leroy next to Galveston Conference Center. Both due to the efforts of Don Mize.
2008	Deaf youth and faculty at Texas School for the Deaf start a Surf Club.

Bibliography

Allen, Gordon L. "Athletics: Leroy Colombo." *The Silent Worker* 38.9 (1926): 418-419. Web. N.d.

Andrews, Jean F., Irene Leigh, and Mary T.Weiner. *Deaf People: Evolving Perspectives in Psychology, Education, and Sociology.* Boston: Allyn, 2004. Print.

—. "Leroy Colombo: The Deaf Lifeguard of Galveston Island Part I: The Early Years (1905-1943)." *East Texas Historical Journal.* 48.2 (2010): 85-109. Print.

—. "Leroy Colombo: The Deaf Lifeguard of Galveston Island Part II: The Later Years (1943-1974)." *East Texas Historical Journal* 49.1 (2011): 9-34.

Babb, Stanely E. "Looking Backward." N.d. *Leroy Colombo Papers.* MS Rosenberg Lib., Galveston.

Belfiglio, Valentine J. *The Italian Experience in Texas: A Closer Look.* Austin: Eakin P, 1995.

"Benefit Dance To Send Colombo to Biloxi." *Galveston Daily News* 29 July 1928: 3. Print.

"Born On the Island." *Galveston Daily News*, 8 June 1956, 5. Print.

"Body of Newspaper Circulation Man is Sent to Dallas." N.d. *Leroy Colombo Papers.* MS Rosenberg Lib., Galveston.

Carroll, Cathryn, and Sue M. Mather. *Twenty-Six Tales of Genius, Struggle, Perseverance and Heroism, Movers and Shakers: Deaf People Who Changed the World*. San Diego: Dawn Sign P, 1997.

Cartwright, Gary. *Galveston: A History of the Island*. Fort Worth: Texas Christian UP,1991.

"Car Plunges Off Seawall," *Galveston Tribune* 4 October 1962: 1. Print.

"Colombo to Race Fort Worth Swimmer in Gulf." *Galveston Daily News* 26 Sept. 1947. Print.

"Colombo is Victor in Marathon Swim Event Held in Gulf." *Galveston Daily News* 23 Aug. 1923: 1. Print.

"Colombo Departs Today For Meet." *Galveston Daily News* 15 Aug. 1926. Print.

"Colombo Makes Another Rescue." N.d. *Leroy Colombo Papers*. MS Rosenberg Lib., Galveston. Print.

"Colombo Winner of S.T.C. Swim Crossing and Johnson Second and Third In the Five-Mile Race." N.d. *Leroy Colombo Papers*. MS Rosenberg Lib., Galveston. Print.

"Colombo To Race Fort Worth Swimmer In Gulf." N.d. *Leroy Colombo Papers*. MS Rosenberg Lib., Galveston. Print.

"Crockett Soldier Drowns in Gulf." *Galveston Daily News* 5 May 1946: 15 A.

Deaf-Mute Saves 106 Lives in Fifteen Years." *Houston Press* 7 July 1936.

"Deaf Takes Famed Lifeguard." *The Deaf American* 1974, 23. Print.

"Deaf Mute Will Try Plane Drop to Get Hearing." N.d. *Leroy Colombo Papers*. MS Rosenberg Lib., Galveston. Print.

"Eight Tanned Boys Save Many Lives." N.d. *Leroy Colombo Papers*. MS Rosenberg Lib.,Galveston. Print.

"870 Swimmers Owe Their Lives To This Man." N.d. *Leroy Colombo Papers*. MS Rosenberg Lib., Galveston. Print.

Evans, Clayton. *Rescue At Sea: An International History of Lifesaving, Coastal Rescue Craft and Organisations*. Annapolis: Naval Institute P, 2003. Print.

Fendler-Brown, Gini, and Max Rizley, Jr. *Galveston Lore, Legend, & Downright Lies*. Austin: Eakin P, 2000. Print.

Flexner, Simon. "The Results of the Serum Treatment in Thirteen Hundred Cases of Epidemic Meningitis." *Journal of Experimental Medicine* 17 (1913): 553-576. Print.

"Four Charged After Affrays On Beachfront Fighting Near Murdoch's Bathhouse." N.d. *Leroy Colombo Papers*. MS Rosenberg Lib., Galveston. Print.

"Game Law Violations Charged Three Men." *Galveston Daily News* 2 Apr. 1941: 4.

Gannon, J. Deaf Heritage: *A Narrative History of Deaf America*. Silver Spring, MD: National Assn. for the Deaf, 1981. Print.

Griffith, Stan. "Fish out of Water." Workers for Jesus. Web. 17 May 2009.

Hardwick, Susan. *Mythic Galveston: Reinventing America's Third Coast*. Baltimore: John Hopkins P. 2002.

Hawes, K. "Museum to honor Galveston lifeguard." *Galveston Daily News* 2 May 2005: A1,3

Hovinga, Sharon Kay Crawford Forestal, and Franna Camenisch. "Remarkable TSD Sports History." *Texas School for the Deaf Sesquicentennial: A Proud Tradition*. Austin: Texas School for the Deaf Alumni Assn. 2010. 624, 626.

—. and Franna Camenisch. *Texas School for the Deaf Sesquicentennial: A Proud Tradition*. Austin: Historical Pub., 2010.

Hunsucker, John L. "Engineering of the Eye and How it Impacts Lifeguard Scanning." World Aquatic Health Conference Seminar 2007. Cincinnati, OH. 2-4 Oct. 2007. Conference Presentation. Web. 24 May 2013.

Jones, Robert L. "LeRoy Colombo—The Lifeguard Who Would Not Quit." *Between Magazine* Apr. 1981: 9-12.

Kelly, Shelly Henly. "Deaf lifeguard makes career of saving lives." *Galveston Daily   News* 9 Mar. 1998: 15A.

Kendall, Kitty, "Swimmer Saves 9808 Lives, But Receives Only Thanks." N.d. *Leroy Colombo Papers.* MS Rosenberg Lib., Galveston. Print.

LaBounty, Woody. "Before Now—Fleischhacker Pool and Its 6 Million Gallons." *Ocean City Bulletin*. Web. 31 May 2013.

Lang, Harry G. *A Phone of Our Own: The Deaf Insurrection Against Ma Bell.*" D.C.: Gallaudet UP, 2000. Print.

Lee, Skip. "Introduction to Lifeguarding and the History and Development of Professional Lifeguards." Ocean City Beach Patrol. 1998. Web. 29 May 2013.

"Leroy Colombo Dares Gulf Waters to Win 15-mile Swim in Fast Time." *Galveston Daily News* 6 Sept. 1927.

"Leroy Colombo Rites Monday." *Galveston Daily News* 14 July 1974.

"Leroy Colombo Gets $50 Check For Man He Rescued in Bay." N.d. *Leroy Colombo Papers, 1905-1974, 1928-1980*. MS Rosenberg Lib., Galveston. Print.

"Leroy Colombo Winner in Australian Pursuit Race."
     N.d. *Leroy Colombo Papers*. MS Rosenberg Lib.,
     Galveston. Print.

"Leroy Colombo Swim Center Building Name Unveiled
     During the 150th Celebration."
     *Lone Star: Journal of the Texas School for the Deaf,
     1856-2006* Summer (2006): 16-17.

"Lifeguard Saves Four From Surf." *Galveston Daily
     News* 1 Apr. 1945: 23.

"Local Swimming Ace Faints Before Giving Up in 14-Mile
     Swim Held at Biloxi, Mississippi." N.d. *Leroy
     Colombo Papers*. MS. Rosenberg Lib., Galveston.
     Print.

"Mahan May Try Air Ride to Restore His Hearing." *San
     Antonio Light* 22 June 1927.

McComb, David G. Galveston: *A History*. Austin: U of
     Texas P, 1986. Print.

McWhirter, Norris, and Ross McWhirter. *Guinness Book
     of World Records*. New York: Sterling, 1976. Print.

Mitchell, Christie. "Treasure Isle Combings." N.d. *Leroy
     Colombo Papers*, MS Rosenberg Lib., Galveston.
     Print.

Panara, Robert, and John Panara. *Great Deaf
     Americans*. 1ST ed. Silver Spring, MD: T. J. Pub.,
     1983. Print.

Price, Granville. "Deaf and Dumb Youth Wins 10-mile Race in Gulf" *Galveston Daily News* 7 Sept. 1925.

Schuchman, John S. *Hollywood Speaks: Deafness and the Film Industry*. Urbana: U of Illinois P, 1988. Print.

"Sharks Invade Houston for Swim." *Galveston Daily News* 1 Aug. 1931: 7.

Showers, Bill. "I've Got Sand in My Toes—Colombo." *Galveston Daily News* 4 Dec. 1970: 9A.

Sophian, Abraham. "Reports Epidemic in Dallas and Other Texas Cities Practically Stamped Out." *New York Times* 4 Feb.1912: 14.

Skomal, Lenore. *The Keeper of Lime Rock*. Philadelphia: Running P, 2002.

"S.T.C. Members Make Plans for Successful Summer Beach Season," N.d. *Leroy Colombo Papers*. MS Rosenberg Lib., Galveston. Print.

Stevenson, Jim. *Wildlife of Galveston*. Galveston: VanJus P, 1999.

"Surf Toboggan Club Promotes Swimming on Gulf Coast." *Galveston Daily News* 6 Feb. 1927: 6.

Taylor, Heber, and Scott E. Williams. "Seawall Memorial Sought for Legendary Lifeguard." *Galveston Daily News* Feb. 2008: B-1.

Texas School for the Deaf Annual Report (2008-2009). "New Surf Club Established With Expedition School." Governing Board Minutes, Summer, 2009.

"Two Negroes Are Drowned Here In Waters of Bayou." N.d. *Leroy Colombo Papers*. MS Rosenberg Lib., Galveston. Print.

Vernon, McCay, and Jean F. Andrews. *The Psychology of Deafness: Understanding Deaf and Hard of Hearing Students*. White Plains, New York: Longman, 1990. Print.

Vernon, McCay. "Sociological and Psychological Factors Associated with Profound Hearing Loss." *Speech and Hearing Research* 12 (1969): 541-563. Print.

Weems, John Edward. "Galveston Hurricane of 1900." *Handbook of Texas*. Web. Texas State Historical Assn. 24 May 2013.

"Work of Leroy Colombo Praised." *Galveston Daily News* 14 Mar. 1928.

Wright-Gidley, Jodi, and Jennifer Marines. *Galveston: A City on Stilts*. Portsmouth, NH: Arcadia, 2008. Print.

Book Club Discussion Questions

1. Explain how Leroy's relationship with his brothers and his mother helped Leroy cope with being deaf.
2. How is it that Leroy Colombo was an excellent lifeguard in spite of being deaf?
3. In what ways did Leroy's parents respond to their son becoming deaf?
4. How did the Deaf community perceive Leroy?
5. How did the older lifeguards in the Galveston Beach Patrol become essential participants in helping Leroy develope into a lifeguard?
6. What was provided for Leroy at the Texas School for the Deaf that he could not obtain in the public school in Galveston?
7. How has Leroy been honored by the communities in (a) Galveston and (b) the Texas School for the Deaf?
8. Why would the Deaf community want to see the term "deaf-mute" removed from an historical marker?
9. What techniques did Leroy use to save a drowning victim?
10. How did Leroy's biography expand your knowledge about American Sign Language and Deaf culture?

www.ingramcontent.com/pod-product-compliance
Lightning Source LLC
Chambersburg PA
CBHW021506090426
42739CB00007B/486